The Great
Disconnect
in Early Childhood Education

The Great
Disconnect
in Early Childhood Education

What We Know vs. What We Do

● ● ● ● ● ● ● ● ● ● ● ● ● ● ● ● ●

MICHAEL GRAMLING

Foreword by Elizabeth Jones, PhD

Redleaf Press®
www.redleafpress.org
800-423-8309

Published by Redleaf Press
10 Yorkton Court
St. Paul, MN 55117
www.redleafpress.org

First edition 2015
Cover design by Jim Handrigan
Cover photograph by Ryan McVay/Photodisc/Thinkstock
Interior design by Dorie McClelland, Spring Book Design
Typeset in Adobe Minion Pro
Printed in the United States of America

Library of Congress Cataloging-in-Publication Data
Gramling, Michael.
  The great disconnect in early childhood education : what we know vs. what we do / Michael Gramling.
      pages cm
  Includes bibliographical references and index.
  ISBN 978-1-60554-399-4 (alk. paper)
  ISBN 978-1-60554-400-7 (ebook)
1. Early childhood education--United States--History. 2. Early childhood education--Social aspects--United States. 3. Child care--United States--History. I. Title.
  LB1139.25.G73 2015
  372.21--dc23
                        2014041252

                                                    U16-06

To my five children, Cotton, Willie, Lauren, Magnolia, and Amelia, who alternately validated and debunked every early childhood theory and every approach to parenting I had ever entertained, and who showed me that my best option was to strap myself in and enjoy the ride.

Contents

Preface

I was a stay-at-home dad in 1979 when I was hired as a classroom teacher at a local Head Start program, even though my only qualifications were that I liked kids and needed a job. Despite my lack of formal training, or perhaps because of it, I did a pretty good job and had a great time. My approach was simply to expose the children to as many different real-life experiences and real objects as I could muster. We planted things, built things, cooked things, climbed things, painted things, cleaned things, imagined things, and took care of living things, including each other. We played games and musical instruments, read a ton of books, and listened to all kinds of music, much of which I brought from home. We explored our neighborhood every day and our community whenever I could hijack a bus. Moreover, I engaged children throughout the day in authentic conversation. (That is to say, I talked to each child like a real person.) I created a climate in which all the children felt like the classroom belonged to them. They could change the schedule to accommodate a particular project, or rearrange the room to support an extended bout of imaginary play. No one was ever forced to participate. Children who preferred solitude could be by themselves.

I hasten to add that I was neither a maverick nor a rebel in my approach. My bosses were my enthusiastic supporters, and many of my colleagues took much the same approach. There was then as there is now an opposing camp who were aghast at what we did. Children needed structure, they said, and they needed to learn the "fundamentals" like letters, numbers, colors, and shapes. Most of all, they needed to learn how to conform to the demands of institutional life. The kind of open-ended operation I was running might be fun, but it did children a disservice and would not prepare them for success in school.

We had no way of proving in my early years of teaching whether what we were doing for children was best or even right. I could not say with any certainty if the children in my classrooms went on to perform any better in school or, as adults, if they were better able to compete in the global economy. But since then, our approach has been vindicated by a great deal of research. What is most fundamental during early childhood, we have learned, is not the alphabet—it is healthy brain development. The brain goes through an intense period of activity that will never be repeated in later years, and the extent and effectiveness of that activity is to a large degree a product of the experiences and conversations to which the child is exposed during the early years. So certain is our profession of this phenomena that programs are springing up all over the country that encourage parents, particularly low-income parents, to talk to their children much more and to give them a variety of experiences to talk about—which makes it all the more puzzling that in modern early childhood classrooms, children are barely spoken to at all.

For the past two decades I have spent most of my time visiting early childhood programs all over the United States, observing classrooms and listening to the concerns of teachers, managers, directors, and principals. I have become intimately familiar with early childhood education as it is actually practiced in the United States, and I have grown increasingly discouraged. What I initially understood to mean that the opposing camp had a lot of followers in the wider world has given way to the stunning realization that the opposing camp has completely won the day. Despite the accumulated knowledge of the past three decades, under the misguided banner of school readiness and accountability, the preschool experience has been reduced to tedious rote learning and strict conformity to routines. It is not that the practices we once held dear have vanished completely—they have become instead the almost exclusive purview of the well-to-do. Judging from the ever-widening achievement gap between rich and poor, it seems to be working quite well for them.

I have therefore devoted a great deal of my time and energy persuading one teacher, one program at a time to give children what they know is best—and there lies the problem. I'm not telling them anything they don't already know. They know child development. They've studied brain research. But they feel—and rightly so—completely constrained by public policy that demands that children be taught in a heavily scripted, incremental manner that flies in the face of everything they know is true.

So I decided to write this book. It is addressed to policy makers who perhaps are not aware of the everyday consequences to children and teachers of learning standards and accountability. It is addressed to teachers, school districts, and Head Start programs who have it within their power to provide the critical experiences and rich discourse children need in spite of the demands of the bureaucracies that look over their shoulders. It is written to parents who are considering enrolling their children in pre-K, Head Start, or child care so that they can make informed decisions about how their children will spend their time during their most formative years.

Childhood only happens once. It is our responsibility to make sure we make the most of it.

Acknowledgments

I want to thank some of the many folks who shared in the development of this book, beginning with my friend and colleague Luis Hernandez, whose generous spirit has provided me with any number of opportunities to say what was on my mind, including the time, shortly after the publication of his own coauthored book *Learning from the Bumps in the Road*, that Luis made the offhand remark that Redleaf Press might be interested in "my stuff." I had a twenty-page article that I had peddled unsuccessfully to various periodicals (who publishes twenty-page articles, anyway?), and I had given up on it, but Luis's comment struck me as a good omen.

I sent the article to Redleaf as an attachment in an e-mail with the subject line "My good friend Luis Hernandez" and was delighted when I heard back almost immediately from Kyra Ostendorf and David Heath, who had taken the time to read an unsolicited article. As it turns out, they don't publish twenty-page articles either, but they encouraged me to turn it into a book, and they have continued to support me throughout the process.

But before the first SASE was licked and sealed, I leaned on my friends for feedback just to find out if they thought my article was any good at all, including Dr. Phil Jos, Joyce Graham, and Ellen Quigley. I learned more than I had anticipated. Their response was positive, their suggestions helpful, but it was from them that I first began to see that what I had to say might provoke some very strong reactions.

I sent the first draft of the book to Dr. Betty Jones, my mentor and professor emerita at Pacific Oaks College from a dozen years earlier, uncertain that she would have the time to read it. But Betty did not just read it, she made it her own. She wrote the foreword, shared the manuscript with her colleagues, and gave me invaluable and detailed feedback. "I read it a second time out loud," Betty explained to me, knowing, I suppose, that I would be curious about the way she was able to be so in tune to the rhythm as well as the content of each chapter. It was not just that her feedback made for a more concise, readable, and theoretically sound manuscript, but the warmth and enthusiasm with which she embraced the project made me begin to believe that I was onto something important.

As it began to dawn on me that my book might be both embraced and castigated by the early childhood profession, I sent the edited manuscript to friend and mentor Dr. Marce Verzaro-O'Brien, the executive director of Training and Technical Assistance Services at Western Kentucky University, for whom I had been employed for over twenty-five years and with whom I continue to work on a freelance basis. She deserved the opportunity, I thought, to know ahead of time that there might be some serious pushback coming down the pike in the near future.

When Marce told me to go for it, the deal was sealed.

The actual finished manuscript, however, could not have been possible without the collaboration, support, and very hard work of my editor at Redleaf, Danny Miller, who is as funny as he is patient and insightful.

But the story of this book began long before I first put fingers to keyboard and hit Save at the end of chapter 1. It is the culmination of a lifetime of work in which I learned about early childhood education—the process as well as the profession—from the bottom up and from the inside out. And for that opportunity I want to thank Colleen Mendel, my boss, my friend, and my mentor for thirty years. She somehow—from the very first time she witnessed me standing on my head in my classroom full of wide-eyed and incredulous three-year-olds—saw in me something I didn't know was there and began a lifelong process of pushing me outside my comfort zone to try things I had not considered possible. She was the first supervisor I ever had who actually meant it when she said she wanted me to learn from my mistakes.

As it turned out, the learning opportunities were many.

My biggest regret is that Colleen passed away before I had a chance to share this book with her and to let her know that her faith in me was well founded.

And finally, Teresa Christmas, who, before she became my wife, was my coteacher in that very same classroom. Shortly after we met, with no small amount of trepidation, I showed her a story I had written, fearful that, not knowing how to let me down easy about my writing, she might decide instead just to let me down easy about everything else. She read it. She handed it back to me. "Keep writing," she said. Since that time not a story I've shared with anyone—in e-mail, on Facebook, or in manuscripts to various publishers, including my good friends at Redleaf—has seen the light of day without her feedback, sometimes tearfully supportive, sometimes adamantly critical, but always passionate and always right on target.

There would be no book without her.

Foreword

by Elizabeth Jones, PhD

"One fine morning in the mid-1960s . . .", this book begins, "Head Start . . . was launched with overwhelming support and goodwill. . . . Head Start declared that it could actually eradicate poverty in the United States."

That promise has been not been kept.

At that mid-twentieth-century time of civil rights activism in America, deprivation and disadvantage were identified as social justice problems to be addressed by the federal government. Head Start was a multifaceted program designed to reach young children and their low-income families with compensatory education and health services. It required parent involvement; parents participated in the classroom and on committees and boards, and were encouraged to continue their own education. For many, Head Start became a job and career opportunity, as they became teachers and directors in early childhood programs.

What did it do for the children? Not so much.

What Went Wrong?

A "head start" for four-year-olds was a good idea. But every good idea comes with its own risks. The big risk for Head Start, in its programs for young children, was the imposition of testing as the measure of success.

Large-scale funding demands accountability. As a publicly funded program, Head Start became accountable at a level previously rare in early childhood education. An idea that moves into the public arena has to be simplified in order to gain voter support. And so standardized research-based evidence of children's learning was sought to assure us that our tax dollars were being well spent. Numbers of all sorts were expected to serve as shorthand for learning. Testing became big business. "Teaching to the test" took over.

What Was Early Childhood Education Like before Federal Funding?

Before Head Start, most early childhood programs had been left alone to develop practice-based theory. Part-day preschools typically served middle- and upper-income families able to pay tuition or educated mothers coming together to initiate parent cooperatives. Many were lab schools serving university communities and created to study the behavior of young children. They were autonomous, without accountability to public funding sources.

In these preschools, early childhood educators and researchers discovered a great deal about young children as learners. Guidelines for developmentally appropriate practice were professionally developed and widely implemented. They made it clear that young children are active learners who need to practice initiative—to play.

That's not a familiar view of schooling. All adults have been to school and know how it works. They assume that if children are to learn, teachers must teach. Our familiar image of teaching is telling, by the lecture method in a group. And learning therefore requires listening and practicing—drilling on assigned tasks. Knowledge gets measured by testing on facts and skills.

But that's not how four-year-olds learn. (Eight-year-olds don't learn that way either, but they've mostly learned to sit still and shut their mouths.) If the voting public, including parents, is to support public funding that claims to leave no child behind in the race to the top, then its programs need to appear credible on the surface.

However, treating young children as students expected to meet uniform goals contradicts everything we know about development in early childhood.

The Knowledge Gap

The gap between rich and poor children in America hasn't narrowed, as promised; it has widened. Public funding has backfired. Preschools funded for the poor are caught in the canned curriculum and testing mania. The preschool experiences of privileged children are more likely to be developmentally appropriate (building on what all recent research now verifies) than are the preschool experiences of young children who start out behind—and fall further and further behind. Test scores continue to reflect the fact that poor children really are disadvantaged, deprived in home, in neighborhood, and in preschool of the great variety of activities and choices and adult conversation and encouragement that are built into resource-rich environments. Early intelligence grows through choices and complexity and self-esteem and negotiating with others—not through memorizing prescribed lists of facts.

The pages that follow provide lots of evidence of how best to support children's intelligence.

Can the Gap Be Closed?

This book provides both a compelling historical analysis—this is what went wrong—and a new vision for the future—this is what can make it right. It doesn't prescribe a how-to fix, but it does demonstrate, through real-life stories, what's possible. The author moves from pessimism to optimism, despair to hope, with stories of real people trying out real theories. Broken promises can be mended, we are assured, if we commit to the challenge of putting theory into practice, ideals into reality.

Shortcuts are not the answer. Children are intelligent human beings, ready and eager to learn in the company of grown-ups. They can't be standardized. They can be respected and invited to grow. This is what it looks like—and if we are really committed to social justice, then this is what we need to be doing.

From the vision of Head Start as an opportunity for social change to the reality of school readiness testing, Michael Gramling invites us to reflect with him on the story of sixty years of early childhood education in America and to share his vision of an adult-child community of colearners. Can a developmentally appropriate early childhood program build on individual children's strengths, ensuring that they really do learn, while providing valid data for assessment? Can it have a genuine impact on the cycle of poverty? Michael assures us: yes.

Chapter 1

America Discovers Poverty

One fine morning in the mid-1960s, unable to ignore for a moment longer the relentless drumbeat of the civil rights movement, the insulated and comfortable citizenry of the richest, most powerful country in the world awoke to discover injustice and suffering in their midst. Quite suddenly, and for a very brief period of time, the human face of poverty became the subject of choice for the national magazines that both shaped and reflected the popular culture of the day. On coffee tables all across America appeared grainy black-and-white images of the distended bellies of children living in the Mississippi Delta, of soot-streaked faces staring vacantly at the camera from the front porches of Appalachian shacks, and of listless inner-city children in diapers clutching bottles on the cracked linoleum floors they shared with the neighborhood rats.

In the 1960s, a decade in which publicly financed kindergarten was optional and the explosion in child care and preschool still barely on the horizon, most children of poverty encountered the educational system for the first time around the age of six. Unlike their middle-class competitors, these children were coming to school hungry—but no one was serving breakfast, and there really was no such thing as a free lunch, not even in school. Most of these children had spent their critical early years without ever having seen a doctor or a dentist; they were malnourished, anemic, plagued by chronic ear infections and parasites; they had received not a single immunization; and their baby teeth were painfully decayed. All too often, untreated and undetected vision and hearing problems had deprived these children of sensory stimulation crucial to the developing brain, causing cognitive and language delays that would be very difficult to overcome as they grew older.

Head Start Is Born

Confronted with these harsh and inexcusable inequalities, the nation responded with both indignation and compassion. Driven by nothing more than the human impulse to relieve suffering and a fundamental sense of fair play, a bipartisan consensus in Congress emerged that said it was our collective responsibility to level the playing field. In 1965 Head Start, the federal program that currently provides basic health, nutrition, education, and developmental services to over a million low-income children from birth to age five, was launched with overwhelming support and goodwill.

Although the Democratic politicians who pushed Head Start through Congress, including Lyndon B. Johnson and Bobby Kennedy, saw Head Start as having the potential to make a lasting impact on the American social and economic landscape, for the American public there was not necessarily a political agenda or grand social engineering attached to the new federal program. People of almost every political persuasion supported Head Start simply because it was the right thing to do.

Following the debut of Head Start, one by one, states began providing their own versions of early childhood education for low-income children (dubbed pre-K to indicate that, unlike Head Start, these programs were explicitly and narrowly focused on preparing children for kindergarten). By 2012, according to the National Institute for Early Education Research, forty states plus Washington DC offered pre-K programs for four-year-old children deemed at risk for failure by reason of income (Barnett, Carolan, Fitzgerald, and Squires 2012).

Impossible Expectations

Poverty, of course, has not gone away, and children need early childhood education now more than ever. But the collective good-will that has supported unparalleled growth and funding for Head Start and the expansion of early childhood education by state legislatures during the last five decades has largely dissipated. Funding for state programs has declined steadily since 2002, culminating in a record-breaking drop in 2011 to 2012 of $500 million (Barnett, Carolan, Fitzgerald, and Squires 2012). For the first time, the debate over funding for Head Start and pre-K has taken on a completely different character, with garden-variety bickering over how much to spend giving way to substantial questions about whether these programs are worth having at all.

True, the ranks of those who would not spend a dime of their tax money to assist the poor in any fashion have grown considerably, but they have been joined by serious critics across the political spectrum who say that Head Start and school district pre-K programs have failed to deliver on their promise and should be unceremoniously retired.

But what was that promise? Perhaps the greatest contributor to the public sense of disappointment in Head Start has been the program's inability to define itself. President Obama, for example, continues to refer to early childhood education and Head Start as an investment in America's future (Hudson 2014). This carefully crafted phrase on the one hand invites various constituencies with competing and often opposing agendas to project on it whatever meaning best suits their goals and worldview, but on the other hand guarantees disappointment and resentment when those goals are not accomplished.

The starkest example of impossible expectations and failed agenda was set into motion before the original Head Start Act was even signed into law. Perhaps fueled by a desire to oversell a program that was basically about human decency and could have stood on its own as an important piece of the social safety net, the architects of Head Start upped the ante considerably in statements to the press and to Congress.

In the giddy heyday of Lyndon B. Johnson's Great Society, Head Start declared that it could actually eradicate poverty in the United States.

Language Deprivation

From our vantage point today, the pronouncements that Head Start could break the cycle of poverty seem hopelessly naive. Now that the War on Poverty has proven to be as successful as the War on Drugs, Head Start seems to many to be little more than an anachronistic monument to good intentions and wishful thinking. The persistence of poverty in the face of billions of dollars invested in Head Start and state preschools over five decades, as well as the fluctuations in the severity of poverty as the economy grows and shrinks, is fairly compelling evidence that poverty is systemic and not simply a function of the lack of early childhood education.

It would be unfair and inaccurate, though, to dismiss Head Start and preschool in general as nothing more than a haven for do-gooders or a soft landing place for politicians wishing to avoid the minefield of extraordinarily difficult options that might be needed to actually address poverty. The pioneers of early childhood education for children in poverty really were onto something very important.

It had long been known, for example, that early childhood was an especially critical period in the life of every individual. Swiss psychologist Jean Piaget had demonstrated earlier in the twentieth century that the ways in which human beings think and process information during early childhood was significantly different than how we accomplish these same tasks during the school years and throughout adulthood. Piaget and almost every other theorist in human development agreed on the basic principle that experiences during early childhood could affect outcomes for the rest of a person's life.

The founders of Head Start quite correctly targeted early childhood as *the* window of opportunity to make lifelong changes in the lives of children. It made sense, and still does, that if poor children whose early experiences in home and neighborhood were substantially different from those of middle-income children were provided experiences that closely replicated those of their more affluent counterparts, then these children could also succeed.

As Head Start expanded, as preschool and child care became commonplace, and as the money spent on them grew exponentially, the nascent field of child development exploded, and research into critical questions gathered considerable impetus. Was there a physiological basis for the differences in thinking between very young children and children seven and older that had been observed by Piaget? Can we identify those specific early experiences that predict success? Can these experiences actually be provided by institutions such as Head Start and public school systems?

So far the answers to these questions are . . .

"Yes."

"Yes, and . . ."

"Yes, but we have failed to do so."

Piaget's observations have been completely validated by modern brain research not available to Piaget himself. (Rapid growth in synaptic density in human infants was first identified in the 1980s [Bruer 2014].) The human brain in early childhood engages in intense activity in which essentially it wires itself. Brain cells are connected. Pathways are developed. The quality of the child's early experiences determine how well and how thoroughly the wiring is completed; however, at around age five or six, at exactly when Piaget said the change would occur, the job is for the most part over, for better or worse, especially in those parts of the brain responsible for language development. The *developing brain* that from birth takes in information at lightning speed from multiple and simultaneous sources becomes at age six the *linear brain* that each of us brought with us to first grade and that we are still using to decipher this chapter.

And the specific experiences and conditions that support healthy brain development in early childhood? Well, certainly adequate nutrition is a primary need for the developing brain, as is rich sensory input, including physical touch, and an environment reasonably free from toxins and trauma. An adult can endure long periods of isolation and deprivation and can suffer all sorts of emotional and physical trauma, and still experience full recovery once more favorable conditions are restored. The developing brain from birth to five, however, cannot, and any number of risk factors can cause damage that is very difficult to overcome (Center on the Developing Child 2007).

But for one glaring exception, Head Start and to a lesser extent school system pre-K programs have done a very good job in removing risk factors and providing environments to low-income children that foster healthy brain development. That glaring exception, unhappily, is the ability to provide rich or even adequate environments that support language development. While there are many specific experiences that influence brain development, the starkest contrast between poor and more affluent children is *experience in hearing and using language.* Simply stated, compared to their more affluent counterparts, many low-income children from birth to five suffer language deprivation. For a variety of reasons, their families do not provide the same quantity of language as do more affluent families, so that in terms of sheer number of words, the middle-income child will have been exposed to over three times the language that the child in poverty will hear by the time she reaches school age (Hart and Risley 1995), at which time the window of opportunity for language development that is open wide during the child's early years begins to close.

But for one glaring exception, Head Start has done a very good job in removing risk factors.

Can You Say, 'Am-phib-i-an'?
Instructional Mode vs. Communication Mode

Consider the middle-income professional father who takes his four-year-old on a walk in the park. Unaware of the incredible capacity of his child's developing brain to absorb information, Daddy provides his son with some linear, incremental instruction. Operating in *instructional mode,* he points out a specimen of native wildlife to his son.

"That's a frog," he explains. "A frog is an amphibian. That means it can live on the land and in the water. Can you say, 'am-phib-i-an'?" At supper that night, the daddy exhorts his child to "tell Mama what you learned today," and after some amount of coaching, the child repeats the lesson. Both parents beam. Dad is a great teacher. Their kid is a genius.

Actually, if the child had to rely on this level of teaching to support healthy brain development and to prepare for future success, this youngster would begin school with the receptive vocabulary of an overachieving chimpanzee. Daddy, in instructional mode, has provided his offspring with a single noun: amphibian. Perhaps tomorrow he will provide another. Fortunately for the child, neither parent visits instructional mode very often. Instead, they remain in *communication mode* almost all of the time, albeit completely oblivious to the rich language experiences they are providing for their child.

During that same evening meal, for example, in communication mode, Mom tells Dad the story about her trip to the mall to return a small appliance. It's bad enough to discover that a simple piece of equipment is defective the moment it is put into operation, worse yet to endure the tedium of parking lots and lines, but simply unconscionable that the clerk would be rude and would not provide a refund without a receipt. Mom's sister, by the way, just last week returned some defective merchandise to that same establishment—defective merchandise must be their specialty—and had wrangled a refund from that very same customer service desk without a shred of evidence that she had purchased it there. It's just fine if the store needs to establish return policies, but they need to be followed consistently, and now Mom intends to boycott that place of business because it's better for the planet to buy locally anyway.

And so on.

Later that evening, still in communication mode, the parents disagree on what to watch on television: Mom wants to watch a reality TV competition involving would-be fashion designers and runways; Dad wants to watch college basketball. Assertions are made on both sides as to who always has control of the remote and who got their way last time. Evidence is offered as to which show has the more redeeming qualities (creativity versus teamwork) and the relative importance of each program (season finale of the fashion competition, opening round of tournament). Family tradition and career are both invoked ("My dad will ask me if I saw the game" and "My clients love this show, and everyone but me will be talking about it in the morning").

In incremental instructional mode, words drip from the faucet slowly, one noun at a time. "Can you say, 'am-phib-i-an'?" But in communication mode, nouns, verbs, adjectives, and adverbs flow in a mighty torrent. As the child listens to these stories and conversations, inside his developing brain synapses are firing, new pathways are constructed, neurons are connected, and words are added to the child's vocabulary as fast as they are heard. But acquisition of a larger vocabulary is only part of what is going on. The child, *without any intentional effort*, takes in not only the content of the discussion, but the way ideas are presented—the complex sentence structure, digressions, and irony employed during the mall story; the manner in which arguments are framed, proven, and refuted during the television discussion; and how solutions are negotiated.

By simply listening to these conversations and thousands more like them from birth through age five (including and especially during infancy), the children of affluent, well-educated America acquire communication and critical-thinking skills that will last a lifetime. These are the very skills that will be called upon when the time comes to take the standardized tests in third grade that first sort out the winners and the losers; the skills that will be called upon when a research paper is assigned in high school; and again when Harvard asks for an original essay on a scholarship application.

School may be the place where young people go to become educated, but make no mistake about it, school is a deadly serious cutthroat competition that will determine a child's success in life at a very early age. Percentile rankings on fourth-grade achievement tests will correlate highly with scores earned in tenth grade, drop-out rates, enrollment in postsecondary education, career opportunities, lifelong earning power, and even incarceration rates (Chavous 2012).

That said, the ability to communicate effectively is perhaps the single most important skill a person can develop for success in school and success in life. It is acquired in the developing brain during the child's early years almost exclusively by listening to other human beings communicate. The level of proficiency in communication any individual might achieve is directly related to the quality of communication the child is exposed to in early childhood.

Discourse in lower-income homes can also be quite rich. Words are free, after all. But in too many homes, the children of poverty are not exposed to anywhere near the quantity or quality of language as their middle-income competition. The National Association for the Education of Young Children (NAEYC) puts it this way: "On average, children growing up in low-income families have dramatically less rich experience with language in their homes than do middle-class children. They hear far fewer words and are engaged in fewer extended conversations. *By 36 months of age, substantial socio-economic disparities already exist in vocabulary knowledge"* (NAEYC 2009, emphasis mine). Anne Fernald at Stanford University has since demonstrated that the language gap between low-income children and more affluent children is significant and is measurable by eighteen months (Fernald, Marchman, and Weisleder 2012) and if not remedied is highly resistant to intervention after age five.

It's important to say, in defense of families (low income or otherwise) not providing rich language, that our current understanding of language development seems to equate verbosity with quality. In truth, counting words to measure discourse is sort of like counting notes to measure the quality of a Mozart symphony. In doing so we give no credence to families or cultures that are taciturn

The ability to communicate effectively is perhaps the single most important skill a person can develop.

or plainspoken. Likewise, our assumption that children or adults who use large vocabularies are better communicators is open to question. For example, Ernest Hemingway, a writer openly contemptuous of his contemporaries who used large vocabularies and complex sentence structures, won the Nobel Prize in Literature and the Pulitzer Prize for Fiction with the *The Old Man and the Sea*, a book that uses the vocabulary of an average eighth grader. Although early exposure to rich discourse is critical, clearly our ability to measure the *quality* of that discourse is crude at best. In fact, one could argue that vocabulary is nothing more than the secret handshake of the well educated and the high value placed on vocabulary in school (Rich 2013) is just another way the deck is stacked against children in poverty.

That said, the correlation between rich discourse and school success is real, and if words spoken are so important, why then do parents struggling in poverty not provide them at the same rate as more affluent families? One obvious reason is the parents' own education. These are parents who collectively are more than five times as likely to have dropped out of high school than their affluent competitors (Rumberger 2013) and have scores on standardized tests significantly below those of their more affluent competition (National Center for Education Statistics 2013). For these reasons, the kind of vocabulary used by Mom in her mall story simply is not available to many parents in poverty. One could also argue that parents in poverty are less able to provide the same breadth of experience—museums, the theater, or even the beach—that is taken for granted by higher income families.

But exposure to language can be provided through quite ordinary experiences as well. One need look no further than the language-rich discussions described earlier about exchanging merchandise and watching television to see how that is possible. Children do not have to go to the Smithsonian to be exposed to rich discourse; the grocery store will do just fine. But even the family trip to the grocery store can take on a very different quality for people living in poverty. Some families strap their one-year-old and three-year-old into the built-in child safety seats of the family SUV and head off for the store. During the trip, except for the occasional admonition to "quit teasing your sister," they may ignore their children during the entire journey. They do converse with each other, however, and the three-year-old immersed in his video as well as the one-year-old facing the rear, sucking on her pacifier, take it all in while not appearing to pay the slightest attention.

Other families, though, strap their two children into the back-seat of their '91 Ford Tempo, in car seats provided by the county health department. In the front seat, the mom sorts through the coupons in silence and calculates the amount of money still available on her EBT card. While she worries about how she'll afford school supplies with the little cash she has on hand, Daddy wonders if the bald tire with the slow leak still has one more trip left in it. Despite his preoccupation with the tire, Daddy starts to tell a story to Mama about something his boss said at work, but he never finishes—his attention is diverted by the cop he spots in his rearview mirror.

Mom sees it, too. They both know the left rear brake light is out and that their insurance is expired. Both children are shushed while the parents anxiously scan the strip malls and fast-food joints, looking for a place to escape the scrutiny of the police officer who, unbeknownst to them, has already confirmed to his satisfaction that their tags are up to date but is currently running a check to make sure the tags weren't stolen. At the entrance to the drive-through restaurant, Daddy signals right, turns the steering wheel abruptly and, without having to tap the brake until safely in the parking lot, successfully avoids what might have been a most unpleasant encounter with law enforcement.

In their interactions with police, cashiers, landlords, teachers, doctors, social workers, bill collectors, and bosses, parents living in poverty always have one brake light out and expired insurance. Much of everyday life is consumed with trying to figure out how to accomplish simple daily tasks that people with money take for granted. And while these parents provide excellent role models for resourcefulness, critical thinking, and problem solving, language modeling is not often a strong point.

All of which seems to lend credence to the premise advanced by pundits and demagogues of certain political persuasions that poverty is nothing more than a function of poor parenting, whatever the reason or excuse. If it is true that children are deprived of language during their crucial early years and are therefore likely to remain in poverty themselves, so the argument goes, then shouldn't parents be held responsible? Aren't poor people in fact to blame for being in poverty?

Not at all. The United States of America makes no claim that its citizens—regardless of the level of their educational attainment—are guaranteed a job that pays a living wage, even if they attended a high-quality preschool, had language-rich experiences during early childhood, and graduated from college. Both unemployment and service economy jobs that do not pay a living wage are understood to be necessary pieces of the economic machine. At any given time, upward of 25 percent of the US workforce will find themselves in one of these two groups—unemployed or not earning a living wage—fewer during good economic times, more during hard times. (Look up Census Bureau data for any year. See how many people are unemployed and how many are in service economy jobs. Or, better yet, see how many are not even in the workforce.)

What the United States does guarantee, however, is an education.

Thomas Jefferson, Benjamin Franklin, James Madison, and all their pals believed not only that every person has the right to an education but that it is the responsibility of government to ensure that everyone gets one. In a democratic society, ordinary citizens need to be informed about issues; they need to be able to make well-considered decisions, to engage in problem solving and critical thinking; they need to have the tools to communicate their views and to evaluate the opinions of others.

In that light, education is not about income at all but about the quality of life for every individual. It is of equal value to cab drivers—15 percent of whom held college degrees in 2010 (McGuinness 2013)—baristas, bartenders, cashiers, and hotel housekeepers. Education is worthwhile to artists, writers, flight attendants, homeless people, unemployed people, and people who work for nonprofits for half of what they could make working on Wall Street. Education is a right for those who are born into poverty, for those who fell into poverty when the economy crashed in 2008, and for those who will suffer the same fate the next time it crashes.

The fact that attendance in a state-approved educational institution is mandatory for children in this country is clear evidence that it is the responsibility of the government that so mandates to provide it. The parents living in poverty who are unable to provide language-rich environments for their children and have no understanding of the link between rich language and brain development are therefore no more to blame for their children's difficulty in school than the professional parents with MBAs who have no understanding of congruent triangles and are unable to help their tenth graders with geometry homework.

The failure of early childhood education in the United States is not that it has failed to lift children out of poverty. The failure of early childhood education in America is that it has failed to educate.

Parents at every income level expect that if they send their children to school, including preschool, then people who have expertise in their given fields will provide their children with a high-quality education. It became clear in the 1990s that language-rich experience was the missing piece that could be provided by an effective child development program to make lifelong differences in the lives of the children of poverty. Since then, one would naturally expect teachers to interact with children and with one another in communication mode throughout the day and to share strategies with parents for doing the same in their own homes.

It has never happened.

The failure of early childhood education in the United States is not that it has failed to lift children out of poverty. The failure of early childhood education in America is that it has failed to educate.

Chapter 2

The Accountability Trap

Gather a hundred early childhood teachers in one room anywhere in the United States and ask them for a show of hands if they have heard of Jean Piaget.

Vygotsky?

Erikson?

Dewey?

Hands will go up. Heads will nod in the affirmative. Recognition will appear on almost every face.

How about Ralph Tyler?

Blank faces.

There is really no reason why this particular gathering might recognize Ralph Tyler—except that he has had a more profound impact on the daily practice of early childhood education than nearly all early childhood theorists combined.

Ralph W. Tyler, the "father of the performance objective," was a man who himself knew nothing about early childhood nor did he pretend to. Although his book *Basic Principles of Curriculum and Instruction* (2013), originally published in 1949, catapulted him into the national education spotlight where he reigned supreme throughout the next two decades, it made no mention of early childhood education. It did, however, have a lot to say about how students in grades one through twelve ought to be taught. It was Ralph W. Tyler, long before Stephen Covey (1989) included it among his seven habits, who declared that the educational process should begin with the end in mind.

It seems self-evident now. Wouldn't all teachers need to know exactly what they wanted the student to learn before they began teaching it? Perhaps so, but knowing one's overall goal and reducing it into discrete performance objectives are not necessarily parts of the same process. Tyler revolutionized modern education by redefining the learning objective and by placing assessment at the center of the process. A performance objective, Tyler claimed, must be specific and concrete so that the student's mastery of the objective can be readily assessed.

Therefore, in order to accomplish a broader goal—to teach the basics of chemistry, for example—the instructor must first reduce the goal to a series of specific, discrete, incremental, and observable learning objectives. According to Tyler, only after a clear performance objective is identified should a lesson plan or a learning experience be developed. Once a particular lesson is implemented, the performance of the student is evaluated, using the observable discrete learning objectives as criteria for success or failure. If the objective is accomplished, the next incremental objective is identified and the process begins again. If the objective is not accomplished, the instructor continues to work on the original objective using different lessons until the performance objective is achieved. For example: "The student will identify the nonmetals on the periodic table of elements." If this objective is successfully accomplished, the next incremental objective might be "The student will state the properties of metals and nonmetals." And so on.

It is a process so simple and so completely taken for granted in modern education it seems almost impossible to imagine any other way to teach—except in early childhood, of course. As we have seen, mastery of language in young children does not occur linearly or incrementally. It is not taught, but it is learned almost unconsciously by children through exposure to rich discourse—by listening to adults in their lives using language to communicate with the child and with each other. The developing brain of the child during early childhood is constantly processing information faster and with greater complexity of thought than could possibly be predicted by means of performance objectives. Language acquisition and the development of critical-thinking skills from birth through age five are not processes that occur in readily observable steps. It would therefore be ridiculous to apply Tyler's method to early childhood education.

Wouldn't it?

The Age of Accountability

Politicians and administrators, however, loved the Tyler method because it provided the doorway through which, for the first time, any interested person could enter the classroom and determine scientifically if the taxpayers were getting the most bang for their buck. The reduction of the educational process to observable performance objectives not only made it possible for an instructor to determine if a particular lesson was successful, but now any third party, in theory, could make that same determination just as easily. Furthermore, once all of the micro-steps to any course of study were identified and the capacity to gather and compare data was developed, not only could the effectiveness of a single lesson be assessed, but so could an entire course of study, as could a school and a school system.

It was Tyler's reductionist approach to education that ushered in the "Age of Accountability" and all of its trappings—uniform learning standards at the state and national level for every subject and every age group, standardized testing, and obsessive data collection.

From the beginning, the Tyler method quickly gained acceptance in school systems and in the colleges and universities that prepared teachers. Teachers everywhere began writing lesson plans that began with the phrase "The student will" and concluded with a phrase describing a specific performance objective. The advent of universal learning standards soon made it possible for the instructor to select ready-made performance objectives for any course of study. In no time, canned curricula with prescribed learning activities designed to teach those ready-made objectives became the typical way of educating children.

Perhaps there is good reason to reduce education to measurable incremental learning objectives for children in elementary school and older. There is a certain egalitarianism to a system that requires everyone everywhere to learn the same thing in the same order and to be evaluated in the same way. It is a way of setting high expectations for each student regardless of income level, and, in theory, it gives every student an opportunity to excel based on merit rather than circumstances of birth. Even a policy as heavy-handed and bureaucratically top-heavy as No Child Left Behind—the federal law that mandates testing and penalizes underperforming schools—could be defended by its proponents on these grounds.

Early Learning Standards and Incremental Learning

No Child Left Behind was not intended to measure the academic progress of preschool children, and with good reason. To impose learning standards on early childhood education, one would have to somehow translate the complex processes occurring in the developing brain from birth through five into a set of subjects the child learns at school. Language development, in particular, would no longer be thought of as something the developing brain acquired through experience, but something that had to be taught in incremental steps.

Unfortunately, that seems to be exactly what has occurred.

Consider the first-grade teacher presenting a lesson in language arts. The performance objective for this particular lesson is "The student will correctly identify the noun in simple phrases."

To accomplish the objective, the teacher presents a series of simple phrases to the class and asks the identical questions after each phrase. For example: "*Hot water.* What is hot, class? That's right. The water. Water is a noun."

The red ball, the small mouse, the happy baby, and other examples follow, and the same question is repeated. What is red? What is small? Who is happy? When the teacher is satisfied that her students have grasped the concept, she hands out worksheets in which the children circle the noun. Her assessment of the effectiveness of her lesson is the percentage of correct responses by each child. If the lesson proves successful, tomorrow she will mix things up a bit, using complete sentences, such as "The ball is red." One day at a time, step-by-step, her students will learn to identify the parts of speech in sentences that increase incrementally in complexity.

Cool.

But, in the same building down the hall, the preschool teacher is preparing a lesson in receptive language. Using the identical methodology Tyler had prescribed for the first graders, she leads a small group of seven or eight four-year-old children who share the same performance objective. On her lesson plan, she writes: "The student will correctly identify four prepositions denoting position—*on*, *under, behind*, and *above*."

With a click of the mouse, the teacher can access an activity for teaching these four words to her group of children from the curriculum supplied to her by her school district. She assesses mastery by each student's ability to place objects on, under, behind, and above when directed to do so. She enters their responses into a database that tracks each child's progress and can produce reports complete with bar graphs and pie charts that show each student's and each classroom's achievement at any given moment in receptive language or any other learning or developmental area.

Tomorrow, perhaps, if the lesson is successful, she will work on *out, in, over,* and *below.*

What is most curious about this side-by-side comparison of the first grade and the preschool lesson is how remarkably similar they are. It's great from an accountability standpoint, perhaps, but it is precisely the inability to distinguish between the preschool child and the six-year-old that is at the heart of the failure of early childhood education. The faulty assumptions about early childhood education implicit in these lesson plans include the following:

- Language development for preschool children is a *subject*. It needs to be taught linearly and incrementally, like grammar or arithmetic.
- Four-year-olds are *students*—just like six-year-olds, only shorter. The subject matter needs to be broken down into more easily digestible pieces and spoon-fed, but children in both age groups learn in essentially the same way.

• The job of the teacher is to function primarily in linear instructional mode almost all the time—"Can you say, 'amphibian'?"— and to add to the child's knowledge base incrementally every single day.

Since we know that children who are exposed to rich discourse might achieve a vocabulary of up to twenty thousand words by age five (Marulis and Neuman 2010), let's do the math and compare that to incremental methodology. Let's be generous and assume that four words a day can be taught incrementally using the reductionist approach of the preschool teacher down the hall, and that during each week ten or so new words are also associated with the theme of the week (dinosaurs, farm animals, community helpers, and so on). Let's be extremely generous and assume that words learned by rote are assimilated into the child's vocabulary as efficiently and thoroughly as words heard in context. In other words, we will give equal value to the word learned during the lesson on amphibians as we do to the rich vocabulary overheard during adult communication or heard in conversation with adults. At that rate the child would acquire 30 new words a week, which sounds pretty good until you punch it into the calculator and discover a vocabulary of 1,080 words at the end of a school year. Now assume the child began her early childhood education at age six weeks and was taught words at that rate for five years, and we arrive at a vocabulary of 5,400 words. This is some 14,600 words shy of what might be accomplished by exposing children to rich language and nearly identical to the vocabulary of the child growing up in a language-deprived home.

The uncritical acceptance of Tyler methodology in preschool goes a long way toward explaining the inability of schools to close the language gap. To begin to make a difference in the lives of children, the faulty assumptions described above need to be discarded and replaced by those we know are true:

- Language is not a subject for children age five and under to study—it is an ongoing experience.
- Children enrolled in early childhood education programs are not "students" in the same sense that older children are. They are children, and the way in which they think and learn bears little resemblance to that of older children sitting at their desks.
- Teachers should avoid instructional mode as much as possible and should remain in communication mode most of the day so that the children can acquire the communication skills they so desperately need.

The Great Disconnect

What is most disturbing about the preschool lesson above is that the teachers who implement it along with the administrators and policy makers who require it to be implemented all know better. Many of them have studied child development and brain research or have access to people who have. They know all about language development; how the brain is hardwired to acquire language during the first five years; the importance of early exposure to rich discourse; and the way learning, thinking, and the brain itself change so dramatically during early childhood.

The total disconnect between what early childhood professionals know and what they do is nothing short of astonishing.

The total disconnect between what early childhood professionals at every level know and what they do is nothing short of astonishing. What could possibly account for this strange behavior, for this devoted adherence to failed strategies?

The Reading Wars

Schools. The front lines of the Culture War. The arena of choice for those seeking to push every conceivable agenda, from creationism to birth control. The whipping boy for politicians. The first to be blamed for every social and economic ill, from gangs and drugs to unemployment and the standing of the United States in the global economy.

The last to be funded to actually do anything about it.

Of all the criticism school systems have endured, deservedly or not, the most persistent has been the lack of success in one of its core missions—to teach children to read. "Why can't Johnny read?" the public has demanded to know since the 1950s—even back when the United States was the world leader in almost everything, including education. But the United States no longer automatically walks off with all the gold medals at the Olympics, and its world ranking in literacy now shamefully lags behind places such as Estonia and the Slovak Republic (OECD 2013), and everybody from parents to politicians wants to know why.

It has been a serious enough question to touch off a war all its own—the Reading War—fought by two very persistent and vocal camps, the Decoders and the Whole Language Gang. The Decoders, disciples of Ralph Tyler and his learning objective approach to teaching, believe that the question is a no-brainer. They consider reading to be a technical skill that can be mastered by almost everyone, and if children can't read, it's because no one has taught them the basic skills.

With that theory in hand, the Decoders set out to identify the specific skills children need to read. This is a partial list of what they have come up with so far:

- Children need to know the alphabet. (No telling how much research went into that one.)
- Children need to know that words are made out of sounds: beginning sounds, middle sounds, and ending sounds.
- Alphabet letters stand for those sounds.
- Print is read from left to right. Each group of print represents a word.
- Books have fronts and backs. A person called an author writes the book. A person called the illustrator draws the pictures.

The list can go on and on and on in excruciating detail (even more excruciating than this one), and in fact, it does.

It is an approach to reading tailor-made for the Tyler model.

From the Decoder's point of view, if the student is having trouble deciphering *c-a-t* no matter how many times the remedial reading instructor reads the word out loud to her, blending each of the three sounds ever so slowly, it is because the instructor has not completed an accurate assessment of the child's knowledge and has chosen a performance objective for which the student has not mastered the prerequisite skills. If the performance were assessed accurately, the instructor might identify any number of steps that had been skipped. He might realize that the student was having problems because she did not yet understand that letters represent sounds. Or the student might not understand that a word has a beginning sound, or perhaps she just hasn't figured out which of the many possible sounds that *c* and *a* might make are in play in this particular configuration. According to the Decoders, reading instruction comes down to knowing the micro-steps and assessing exactly where the child stands on the continuum.

The Whole Language Gang is not so sure. They believe that it is quite possible to master every single micro-step in the Decoder's handbook and still not be able to comprehend print or to use it as a means of communication. Acquiring proficiency in language, they insist, is far more important than learning phonics or the conventions of print. Children need to have a sense of story. They need to be exposed to meaningful print in a variety of contexts. Letter sounds are too unpredictable and too unreliable to form the foundation of reading. Teaching phonics confuses more children than it helps. Learning to read, many assert, will occur organically and naturally once children develop a love of books.

Consider, for example, the story of Edward, who decides he wants to learn Spanish in record time in order to impress his bilingual girlfriend who speaks English and Spanish. He learns the Spanish alphabet (nearly identical to his own) and the sounds made by each letter. He already knows all of the conventions of print, so he learns how to interpret Spanish punctuation that to him seems upside down and backward. He studies unfamiliar characters, such as the *tilde* and the *acento*, and learns how they affect pronunciation. In other words, he learns to decode print in Spanish.

At his girlfriend's apartment one evening after a quiet dinner with her and her English-speaking sister, he says, "Have you got anything handy I could read in Spanish?"

Puzzled, his girlfriend hands him a tattered paperback copy of *Cien años de soledad* (100 Years of Solitude) by Gabriel García Márquez.

Without hesitation, Edward begins to read aloud. "Muchos años después, frente al pelotón de fusilamiento, el coronel Aureliano Buendía había de recordar aquella tarde remota en que su padre lo llevó a conocer el hielo. Macondo era entonces una aldea de veinte casas de barro y cañabrava construidas a la orilla de un rio de aguas diáfanas que se precipitaban por un lecho de

piedras pulidas, blancas y enormes como huevos prehistóricos"
(García Márquez 1979).

The two sisters are very impressed. "That was amazing," his girlfriend says on her way to the kitchen.

"But what does it mean?" her sister calls after her.

"Ask Edward," she replies over her shoulder.

The sister looks at Edward expectantly.

Edward flushes deeply. "I have absolutely no idea," he admits.
"I don't speak a word of Spanish."

"So you're like the trained dog I saw on TV last night. His owner
laid out a huge multicolored map of the United States on the stage,
and every time his owner called out a state, the dog sat on it."

"Yes," Edward nods ruefully. "Very much like a trained dog."

Perhaps the Whole Language Gang overstates their case. Probably
most children do need decoding skills—after, of course, they have
been immersed in language from birth to age five or six. But when
decoding print begins at age four and earlier, when it moves early
childhood teachers out of communication mode and into instructional mode for a good part of the day, this is what we get. Pet tricks.

The Whole Language Gang has it right. Obviously, then, the
first and most important step in learning to read and write a language with comprehension is learning how to speak it, not how to
decode it. The more proficient a person becomes in using a particular language, the better that person will be able to read and
to write it. The Decoders would not necessarily disagree. A child
whose home language is Spanish—for example, a child who is just
beginning to learn English—would logically need to have baseline
proficiency in speaking English before attempting to decode print
in English. The Decoders' incremental approach assumes that the
student is an English speaker, not an English-language learner.

What the Decoders do not realize, what is not taken into account in the Tyler model, what is ignored almost entirely by the early childhood community, is this: every single child from birth through age five living in the United States is an English-language learner, including and especially those who grow up in English-speaking homes.

Every single child from birth through age five living in the United States is an English-language learner.

Every child from birth through five learns English (and, indeed, any other language) exactly the same way—by hearing other people use it. Proficiency in reading and writing English is a direct function of proficiency in speaking and understanding English. The prerequisite for reading is not the letter *a*, the prerequisite for reading is the ability to use and understand words. As Lonigan and Shanahan put it so well, "Reading comprehension depends on language abilities that have been developing since birth" (2014, 25).

Preschool children—and in particular the children of poverty— do not need lessons in decoding; they need exposure to rich discourse in English, no matter what the home language. In homes in which English is not spoken, children need to hear their home language at home and they need to hear English spoken in the wider world—the richer the exposure to the home language, the more proficient the child will become in acquiring English as the second language (Tabors 1997).

The Decoders, with their readily measurable performance objectives, quickly gained the upper hand in school systems all over the United States, although at first the popularity of the Decoders had little impact on early childhood education. In the 1950s and 1960s, and on into the early 1970s, school started at age six. But as school systems were put on the defensive not only about reading proficiency but the overall decline in academic achievement in science and math as well, policy makers across the country came to a conclusion that would have enormous impact on the children of poverty.

They decided to start school earlier.

The End of the "Child's Garden"

Kindergarten, created in Germany in 1840 and transplanted to the United States in 1868, literally translated from German means the "children's garden." It was named and planned by Friedrich Froebel as a place where children can choose to explore their world at their own pace using a variety of hands-on materials. Froebel envisioned a child-friendly environment that accommodates a wide range of learning styles and interests and encourages children to make their own choices. Adults are guides and facilitators who help support intellectual development by participating in children's play. It is a nonlinear and open-ended experience in which children build with blocks, explore art materials, play make-believe, sing songs, plant gardens, take care of pets, laugh, and play.

Schools, on the other hand, if nothing else, are linear, and it seems curious that US policy makers would incorporate that kind of open-ended early childhood education into their factory model of incremental performance objectives and instruction doled out by the credit hour. The fact is, they didn't. They simply imposed the Tyler model on five-year-old children and called it kindergarten.

Crushed under the weight of learning standards and assessments and the heavy emphasis on earlier and earlier proficiency in decoding print, the children's garden of Froebel's dreams withered, and in no time at all, it became the "children's job," until over time it morphed completely into what used to be first grade. Essentially, schools took the unsuccessful strategies that had not produced the desired results for students in grades one through twelve and applied them to five-year-olds, hoping for different results. (Come to think of it, isn't that a definition of insanity?) But starting first grade at age five did not produce the desired outcomes, and schools continued to draw heavy criticism for failing to produce an educated population that measured up to the international competition.

You don't have to be Nate Silver to predict what happened next. That's right. School began at age four.

But there was a new twist to this next incursion of school systems into early childhood education. In the intervening years, the national conversation had shifted from the overall problem of literacy and academic achievement to the more specific issue of the achievement gap between low-income and more affluent children as measured by performance on standardized testing and high school graduation rates. The question had mutated from "Why can't Johnny read?" to "Why can't poor kids read?" After all, they were receiving the same incremental decoding curriculum as their middle-income competitors. But as the children of poverty were moved through the educational assembly line, they not only performed poorly on standardized tests (National Center for Educational Statistics 2013), they were retained at grade level at a much higher rate than their more affluent peers (Rose and Schimke 2102).

Not surprisingly, when a child failed a grade, the response of the school was to have him repeat the exact same instruction that had not worked the first time, hoping once again for a different outcome. When that didn't happen and when as a practical matter it became impossible to have the child repeat the same grade over and over again, these students were simply moved through the system until they reached high school, unable to read or comprehend a simple sentence.

As the achievement gap became a national disgrace, and despite the very good evidence before them that language deficiency was the root of the problem, schools decided instead that since starting school at age five had not worked, then starting school at age four must be the solution—not for all children this time around, but for the most part, just for children in poverty. Although some states and municipalities currently offer "pre-K for all," children deemed "at risk" are still more likely to be the target population for most state pre-K programs. It is mostly for the benefit of these children that school readiness standards have been established and performance objectives identified, and for whom decoding print has become a central objective.

Head Start Surrenders to the Accountability Model

And what of Head Start, the original preschool program for four-year-old children and younger who are poor? Head Start had never been envisioned as a school readiness program; it was a child development program. Unlike school system preschool, the overall goal of Head Start was not school readiness. The overall goal of the program that promised to break the cycle of poverty was something it called *social competence*.

By social competence, Head Start meant that it would provide experiences to support children's social and emotional development, as well as physical and intellectual development. Intellectual development included critical-thinking skills, language development, and communication skills. In contrast to schools in which young children are expected to be quiet and listen most of the day and in which children eat in cafeterias patrolled by lunch monitors whose main job is to minimize conversation during mealtime, Head Start was originally intended to be a program that valued conversation. Children ate lunch in their own classrooms in a relaxed atmosphere designed to foster interactions among children and between adults and children. It was a program in which children and adults talked most of the day.

Head Start was and is a comprehensive program that attends to health, nutrition, and dental needs, and a program that works with families to enhance their dignity and increase feelings of self-worth. It does this by encouraging parents to go back to school, to assume leadership roles in their children's program, to apply for employment within the agency. And, most importantly, it supports parents in stepping up to the plate to assume responsibility for their role as the child's primary educator.

As school systems also took on the job of educating the four-year-old children of families in poverty, they initially looked to Head Start as a model, with its emphasis on health, nutrition, the well-being of the entire family, and its staunch determination to support parents as decision makers. Schools started serving breakfast; they hired social workers; and they gave parents more voice in school governance. But when it came to early childhood education, Head Start for many years was viewed by school systems as an amateurish enterprise, in part because communication was valued so much more than decoding print. So adamant were some of the local Head Start programs that they were *not* a preschool, they did not even display the alphabet on the walls of their classrooms. "We are here to support social and emotional development," they would respond resolutely when questioned about this practice, "not to teach ABCs." (These programs had to be gently reminded from time to time by the Office of Head Start that although they were definitely not supposed to be teaching school, there was no reason to keep the alphabet a secret.) Curricula were frequently homemade; teachers were paraprofessionals recruited from the ranks of parents.

Head Start classroom practice, however, was not completely a make-it-up-as-you-go-along enterprise. It was guided by federal regulations as well as an ever-increasing body of research-based guidelines that were responsive to the very specific needs of very young children. Chief among them was the original rendition of what is still, in its third edition, regarded as the final word in best practices for children from birth to eight: *Developmentally Appropriate Practice* (Copple and Bredekamp 2009), or DAP as it is still affectionately known. DAP is a set of principles and practices developed by the NAEYC that celebrates the developing brain of the preschool child and specifies the ways in which young children are to be supported, nurtured, and respected in classrooms. Hands-on activities, support for autonomy and choice, responsiveness to individual abilities and temperaments, flexibility, kindness, patience, and rich language modeling are among the hallmarks of how DAP suggests that young children be cared for, instructed, and valued.

But DAP is about process, not outcomes, and the time finally came to Head Start when supporting child development was no longer enough. By 1997, thirty-some years into the War on Poverty Head Start had been commissioned to fight, it had become apparent that poverty had won. With its mission still not accomplished, Head Start suddenly found itself in the unfamiliar position of having to justify its existence.

"Exactly how much social competence does a child achieve once he enters your program?" critics wanted to know. "How much dignity? How much self-worth?" When accountability came to Head Start, the program was nearly dismantled altogether. It had no mechanism to demonstrate what it had accomplished for the children of poverty that could be understood and valued within the Tyler paradigm. The descendants and disciples of Tyler put enormous pressure on Head Start to abandon its attempts to provide experiences most critical to the developing brain and to provide instead that which is most easily measured.

In late 1997, held hostage by a hostile Congress and over the strident objections of many within its own ranks, Head Start bet the farm on early literacy. Social competence was replaced by school readiness as the program's overall goal. Learning standards were issued that explicitly required that four-year-old children begin to decode print. Furthermore, programs were mandated to gather and track data on the incremental progress of each child in literacy, language, and math. Within a very short time, Head Start and preschool became indistinguishable from each other.

For the children of poverty, the results have been disastrous.

Chapter 3

School Readiness Goals: When Good Intentions Go Bad

When state school systems and Head Start issued school readiness standards for early childhood education, they used as their template the federal definition developed in the early 1990s by the Department of Education. In much the same way that elementary schools have identified subjects such as reading, math, social studies, and science as their core subject matter, school readiness standards have sliced up early childhood education into manageable parts that can be taught and measured. Although there are variations from state to state, a typical lineup of school readiness goals includes language, literacy, math, physical development, cognitive development, social-emotional development, and "approaches to learning" (a set of guidelines that along with social-emotional development describes how very young children ought to behave in order to be ready for school).

Much to the detriment of young children, the establishment of school readiness standards has caused the early childhood profession to

- equate instruction with assessment;
- confuse child development with early learning; and
- substitute early information for early experience.

Equating Instruction and Assessment

School readiness standards, of course, were never intended to be *taught* like subjects in school. They are simply broad, research-based statements that describe the skills and knowledge typical of students who are successful in school. They may have remained nothing more than that if it were not for the requirements of state and federal agencies that early childhood programs assess and gather data on each child's progress toward achieving those goals.

This mandate for constant assessment does for early childhood education what the chemistry instructor does for his tenth graders. It breaks down each of the developmental and learning areas identified in the standards into sequential performance objectives—the linear micro-steps that are necessary to track each child's incremental progress toward school readiness.

For example, to be successful in school, a child had to be reasonably good with her hands. Or, as the school readiness standard would have it, she must develop "fine-motor skills." No argument with that. It's hard to get through school or life if you cannot successfully button and zip or use utensils, pencils, scissors, and keyboards.

And it is true that specific training (or practice) is needed to master certain manual tasks, such as typing on a laptop, picking a guitar, or surgically repairing a heart valve. But in the typically developing child, the basic manual dexterity that will be required to master those tasks and many others does not need to be taught. Manual dexterity begins to develop at birth as the child uses her hands and fingers to grasp and hold objects. As the child matures, so do her abilities to manipulate objects with her hands.

However, today those in the early childhood profession believe that in order for children to acquire basic manual dexterity (in essence, fine-motor skills), adults must intentionally plan experiences and provide materials in order for these skills to develop. Worse yet, the early childhood profession as a whole seems to be an extremely anxious bunch who worry constantly that the child somehow might not develop fine-motor skills despite everyone's best efforts. They are so anxious that they believe it is necessary to gather, store, and analyze megabytes of data just to be absolutely certain it is happening.

And how is that accomplished? By constantly sampling the child's abilities.

Perhaps it benefits children to have so many adults hovering over their laptops to ensure that children are successful; however, one cannot help but wonder at the incredible accomplishments human beings have achieved with our four fingers and opposable thumbs during the thousands of generations since we first appeared on this planet—all without the benefit of early childhood education and without a single soul tracking our progress from birth to age five.

Are we to believe that beginning in the late twentieth century, human beings must suddenly attend preschool in order to develop fine-motor skills? Did B.B. King attend preschool?

Teaching the Samples

As anxious as folks might be about children making progress, as a practical matter it is impossible to measure the entire range of the child's emerging abilities across all of the school readiness domains. So in order to track progress, the assessment instrument provides specific *samples* of skills and knowledge that are hopefully representative of overall ability. Cutting with scissors, for example, is a favorite way to sample fine-motor skills, although in theory the sample tasks could be almost anything from thumbing through the photos on a smartphone to using a Phillips-head screwdriver.

Unfortunately, in data-driven early childhood education, these samples take on a life of their own so that it is the successful accomplishment of the samples that have come to define the child's school readiness and that measure the ability of the teacher to successfully prepare children for school. How do adults prove the child is making progress in large-muscle development? Have him practice standing on one foot for ten seconds, because that is how the assessment instrument will measure his success. Progress in math? Counting backward from twenty is a skill on the assessment that the child could practice every day.

Hmm. With objectives like these, it is difficult to tell if the child is preparing for success in school or for a roadside sobriety test.

Performance objectives . . . have absolutely nothing to do with how children learn or how their brains work.

Teachers are no fools. If the data gatherers want to know how well the children can accomplish the samples, then it is the samples that shall be taught—relentlessly during the child's entire early childhood experience. Assessment, then, becomes indistinguishable from instruction. School readiness, as it is actually practiced in classrooms all over the United States, has become an ongoing process of

- choosing a performance objective (sample) provided by the assessment;
- implementing a lesson provided by the curriculum to work on the performance objective;
- documenting the child's success or lack thereof; and
- selecting the next sequential performance objective and repeating the process until every performance objective is mastered.

Performance objectives may be a great way to teach geometry, chemistry, or grammar in high school. Unfortunately, they have absolutely nothing to do with how children learn or how their brains work from birth through age five.

"Teaching" Language

Of all the school readiness standards that guide practice in early childhood classrooms, the most egregious are those that address language. The standards in and of themselves are benign. They suggest, for example, that children need to acquire a more complex vocabulary. That's fine. It's also completely redundant and unnecessary. Even a child from a home that uses comparatively little language cannot help but acquire a more varied and complex vocabulary during his early years unless he is locked in a closet for the duration. The question is whether the early childhood program will provide the experiences to maximize the acquisition of that vocabulary. The answer so far is probably not. The four words taught by the teacher in the previous chapter, *in, behind, under,* and *below*, are only samples of the child's expanding vocabulary, but in standards-driven early childhood education, *they become the vocabulary itself*—words that need to be taught so that progress can be documented and data collected.

To appreciate how completely wrongheaded this approach to language has become, consider how the developing brain actually acquires a specific concept—the color blue. Early in her infancy, a few moments after she has entered the world, as she stares into her mother's face, the baby girl overhears various friends and family members remark that she has her mother's blue eyes. (Or alternately, no one mentions a word about eye color except the aunt who never knows when to keep quiet, who exclaims, "Oh dear! She has blue eyes?") When no one knows what else to say, the weather comes to the rescue, and the daddy says, "Wow. We finally have some blue skies for a change." A moment later, the new mother wonders out loud if she'll ever fit into her blue jeans again.

The newborn baby is not long into her childhood when she discovers that fingernails, cars, houses, and all manner of clothing (not to mention the teenage babysitter's hair) might be described as blue, although like blue sky, blue jeans, and blue eyes, they are never the exact same color. Depending on her experiences and her environment, she might encounter bluetick coonhounds, blue jays, the Blues Brothers, and the deep blue sea. Things will sometimes come out of the blue, once in a blue moon. Her favorite book might become *One Fish Two Fish Red Fish Blue Fish*.

With every single encounter with the color blue, more neurons connect; the context of the color blue broadens, and the child's understanding of what is meant by blue deepens. As the child is provided language-rich experiences, she will continue to add context and understanding not only to the color blue, but to literally thousands of other concepts simultaneously. Among those thousands of words will be the rest of the colors in the crayon box, as well as *in, behind, under,* and *below.*

In their groundbreaking 1995 work, *Meaningful Differences in the Everyday Experience of Young American Children,* Betty Hart and Todd Risley point out that by the age of four, children in language-rich homes will hear or, more accurately, overhear up to forty-two million words spoken by family members. Since there are only about one million words in the English language, and since even a very expansive adult vocabulary might consist of thirty thousand words, obviously these children hear the same words over and over and over again. As we can see from the example of the color blue, hearing the same words in various contexts repeatedly is exactly how children learn them. It is therefore impossible to pinpoint precisely where the development of the child's understanding of any particular concept might be at any point in time, or which specific language experiences contributed to the child's understanding.

To an early childhood program intent on gathering data and tracking progress, this understanding of language acquisition is completely unacceptable. What is required instead is simplicity and a total lack of ambiguity. Data-driven programs need to be able to say with certainty how many four-year-olds can identify how many colors in any classroom at any given moment in time. Actual language development on the other hand is cumulative—it is about neurons connecting into an ever-denser web, and it is never as simple as data in and data out.

But data in and data out is exactly the approach taken by reductionist pedagogy. Because the kindergarten teacher's definition of school readiness is that children know all the colors in the crayon box, preschool teachers spend weeks at a time "teaching" the color blue as if it were some invisible and mysterious piece of the electromagnetic spectrum, such as infrared or ultraviolet, that could never be learned through normal experience and that is a prerequisite for learning equally mysterious concepts such as red and yellow. "What color is it?" children are asked a hundred times each day.

So yes, the child is always acquiring a more complex vocabulary, as called for in school readiness standards. The problem is that the rate of expansion of vocabulary slows to a crawl once the color blue becomes a "subject" to be taught. Although the child's developing brain absorbs information like a sponge just waiting to be totally immersed in language, in standards-driven early childhood education, we dispense language with an eyedropper.

But teaching micro-language is only part of the story. Tracking progress and gathering data is equally problematic. As the child's developing brain processes language at lightning speed, the child does not typically demonstrate his true progress by reciting definitions or facts or by naming objects on demand as they are presented to him in lessons. Children will instead demonstrate their ability to use and understand language in unscripted interactions throughout the day. Data gathering, however, has created a classroom culture in which the only language development worth noting is that which is explicitly taught and explicitly repeated by the child.

For example, when three-year-old Maggie and her parents visit her grandma one afternoon, Grandma looks out the kitchen window and exclaims, "Maggie! Look out the window! There's a pretty red birdie in the pear tree!" The three-year-old dutifully peers out the window and looks up at her grandmother quizzically.

"Grandma," she asks, "do you mean the cardinal?"

Grandma gives the parents a dirty look. Have they been teaching this child adult vocabulary just to make Grandma look silly?

No, there had been no performance objective identified nor lesson taught. Daddy did not write a lesson plan that said, "The student will identify the cardinal in the *National Geographic Field Guide to the Birds of North America*." But Mom and Dad know exactly how their daughter learned to identify the bird. That morning, pulling into their driveway with Maggie strapped into her car seat, Mom had noticed a cardinal in the front yard and had pointed it out to Dad.

"Hey, look. A cardinal."

"Yeah. He's beautiful."

That was it. Nothing was said directly to the child. In this household, once the child is strapped into the backseat, after about a half mile or so down the road, she becomes cargo, at least until she starts to fuss about something. But although the three-year-old may be out of sight, out of mind, her developing brain never takes a break. As the family pulls into the driveway, from the backseat Maggie hears that there is something in her yard that her parents believe is worth pointing out to each other. Always curious about what matters to adults, she looks; she sees the bird, hears it called a cardinal, and the adult word for "pretty red birdie" is added instantly to her vocabulary.

Or is it? "Backseat learning" is in fact how a great deal of language is acquired during early childhood. Maggie's parents may think they know exactly when and how she learned the word *cardinal*, but they are mistaken. She has spent the first three years of her life in Kentucky, and it is extremely unlikely that the driveway incident was the first time she had heard the word. Like the color blue that is heard over and over again, the cardinal in the driveway simply added further context to a word she had already experienced. The visit to Grandma's simply provided an unscripted opportunity for her to display what she had already known for some time.

Maggie's parents are pleased that their child knows the correct word for the pretty red birdie. In contrast, her preschool teacher is polite but otherwise unresponsive when Maggie points out a cardinal on the playground. The lesson plan that afternoon is not about cardinals; it is about the performance objectives "big," "bigger," and "biggest." The learning activity provided by the curriculum is to provide children with measuring cups of various sizes and invite them to play in the sand. Three children, including Maggie, are having a great time digging tunnels, building roads, and making sand mountains. The teacher interrupts this play to ask the question, "Which of these cups is the biggest?"

Without even looking up, Maggie replies, "The big one" in a tone of forced tolerance that suggests the question is self-evident and hardly worth the interruption of her play. Maggie's teacher doesn't give Maggie credit for her response and continues to ask the same question until one of her playmates holds up "the big one" and exclaims, "This one!"

But Maggie was right the first time. It is the big one. She has encountered "biggest" in a variety of contexts in her young life. She has heard adults say smallest, fastest, meanest, saddest, loudest, and on and on, and by so hearing, she has learned the rules of grammar that apply when using comparative adjectives. If those who have instituted school readiness standards believe it is somehow necessary and desirable to constantly assess a three-year-old child's language ability, they should also implement systems that encourage teachers to value Maggie's remark about the cardinal and to record samples of everything Maggie has to say. This would include words that are incorrect—words that Maggie has never heard at all, such as *gooder* or *mostest*, because it is those words that demonstrate her knowledge of the rules of grammar, even if she does apply them incorrectly. Other children might use words such as *tooths* or *hitted* that by their very incorrectness demonstrate the child's understanding of how plurals and past tense are formed. All of these rules of grammar will be taught formally and incrementally in second grade, but much younger children exposed to rich language already know how to apply those rules in everyday speech.

The ability of children to display their understanding of adult language in natural, unscripted settings cannot be better illustrated than by the true story of the two parents sitting on the living room sofa, deep in conversation, sharing their anxieties about their teenage daughter—all the while ignoring their four-year-old son playing with his cars on the living room carpet. Both parents agree that their daughter has become moody, sullen, withdrawn, and uncommunicative. Maybe it is just a bad case of adolescent angst, but maybe she is suffering from depression. Does she need counseling? Maybe she has an eating disorder. She seems to be putting on some weight lately.

"She's pregnant," the four-year-old interjects matter-of-factly, not bothering to look up from his cars, completely oblivious to the hand grenade he has just lobbed into the middle of domestic tranquility.

Needless to say, the parents are shocked, not at the sudden offhand revelation—obviously the four-year-old has no idea what he's talking about. But where could he possibly have come up with that idea? Has his sister been letting him watch trashy television when she babysits him in the afternoon?

No, she hasn't. As it turns out, he's been watching cartoons every afternoon while his sister has been talking to her girlfriend on her cell phone in the next room. She is, in fact, pregnant.

Does the four-year-old actually grasp the meaning of words such as *sullen, uncommunicative, angst, withdrawn, depression*, and *eating disorder*? Maybe yes, maybe no. He knows that his sister has been sad, upset, and even grouchy. As he listens to his parents talk, he also knows that they are using somewhat unfamiliar words to describe his sister and that they are not happy words, but words that make them worry. Even though his parents have no intention to do so, they manage to scaffold words such as *angst, depressed*, and *sullen* onto his current understanding of human emotion, and have thus begun the process (or perhaps continued the process) of his acquisition of those words in context, words that will be among his twenty thousand when he begins school.

The parents completely underestimated their child's abilities when they discussed the sister's emotional state in front of the four-year-old child on that fateful evening. Likewise, the big sister underestimated him. She never dreamed her little brother was listening to her telephone calls, much less that he could understand her side of some very adult conversations. The teenager and her parents learned the hard way—children from birth are always listening. They are always watching. They understand everything. This child understood completely that

- his sister was pregnant;
- his sister was distraught about her condition; and
- his parents were worried about her but didn't know what was wrong.

That sort of logical reasoning cannot be taught to four-year-olds; it is learned through normal, human interactions. Nor could those vocabulary words be taught in any meaningful way—they are far too abstract. They are learned instead from the "backseat," through direct experience.

Ask anyone to tell a story of something their child says or does that was obviously learned from watching or listening to adults, and it almost always evokes an embarrassing moment. One young mother tells the story of a visit from her mother-in-law who brings a present—a bag of building blocks—for her two-year-old granddaughter. The child tries to build a tower, but when it falls down, the two-year-old exclaims, "Damn!" in frustration.

The child's mama doesn't skip a beat.

"The things that child hears at her nursery school," the girl's mama tsks-tsks to her mother-in-law, all the while making a mental note to be more circumspect next time she spills her glass of wine.

No one would instruct a child to use the word *damn* to express frustration and annoyance, just as no one in his or her right mind would teach a one-year-old to operate the television remote. But nevertheless, there he is, changing the channel in the middle of the Super Bowl.

In part, because families underestimate their child's ability to learn and think is precisely why they inadvertently provide such rich language. They assume they can talk over their child's head with no consequence. Ironically, in standards-driven early childhood education, the child is also completely underestimated, but with results that are completely opposite: he is not provided rich language at all, but is exposed to language in tiny sound bites. For example, in order to "teach" the precocious four-year-old who eavesdropped on his sister words that describe human emotion, the curriculum will provide the teacher with a lesson plan that says, "The child will identify pictures of people who are sad and happy." Since one of the many drawbacks to the use of performance objectives in early childhood is that children are frequently disinterested in performing on demand, the child may or may not complete the task successfully, and the teacher will be concerned that his language skills are lacking.

It is not a good idea for teachers to discuss teen pregnancy and use curse words in front of children in order to provide rich language. It is a very good idea, though, for teachers to pay much less attention to performance objectives and to communicate with one another and with children a great deal more—to talk about their own feelings,

*P*rovide opportunities all day long for children to talk and use those samples as the primary evidence for language development.

ideas, and experiences in ways that are appropriate and authentic and that employ adult sentence structure and adult vocabulary. It would also be wise to provide opportunities all day long for children to talk about whatever comes to mind, to pay attention to what they say and how they say it, and to use those samples of unscripted language as the primary evidence for language development.

Confusing Child Development and Early Learning

Decoding print, naming colors, identifying emotions, and distinguishing "big" and "biggest" are examples of *early learning* that are taught and tracked in preschool, but there are many others. Counting, printing one's name, naming shapes and days of the week are fairly typical early learning objectives as well. One might assume that the entire preschool experience is devoted to early learning.

Not so. A great deal of what is "taught" and tracked in early childhood classrooms is simply *child development*—tasks that are mastered naturally in all human beings as they mature, milestones that are embedded in human DNA that will occur with or without the intervention of parents or preschools.

Consider the milestones any infant will achieve during the first year that would cause the mama to take notice and send a text to the baby's daddy, call her own mom, or post a video on Facebook. (By "the infant," I mean, of course, the first baby. Nobody pays any attention at all to what the second baby does.)

Most of the baby's accomplishments that make mama so proud actually do not represent early learning but are instead purely developmental—they occur in all typically developing children as inevitably as the sun rises in the morning. (*Typically developing* means that the child does not have a developmental disability that would interfere with development and that the child is provided with a reasonably supportive environment in which she is provided basic necessities.) Somewhere along the way all such babies will get their first tooth—a photo op for sure. They will roll over, sit up, crawl, pull up, stand up, and walk.

That is not to say that early learning will not also occur. Depending on her experiences, the baby may also learn to wave bye-bye, hold her own bottle, play peekaboo, or say "Dada." By year two she may even be downloading apps on her mother's smartphone. All of these early learning tasks have a developmental component to them, of course. Holding the bottle and operating the smartphone both require sensory motor skills that all children on the planet develop. What distinguishes these achievements as early learning is the baby's understanding of what to do with the bottle, how to operate the smartphone, and who to direct the word "Dada" to. These skills are not taught but will only be learned by children exposed to those objects or words. A breast-fed baby will toss a bottle out of the crib; a child born in Morocco will not earn an appearance on Facebook by saying "Dada" but may get his own YouTube video the first time he says "baba."

State and federally funded preschool programs include both early learning and child development in the learning standards that they issue to their respective programs. In Head Start, the document that sets forth school readiness standards for all Head Start programs is in fact called the *Head Start Child Development and Early Learning Framework* (Office of Head Start 2011). The *Framework* at least acknowledges in its title that many of the so-called learning standards for young children are not about learning at all—they are about simple biological DNA-driven maturity. Unfortunately, like similar documents issued by state pre-K, the *Framework* makes no distinction between the two in practice.

Teaching early learning objectives, as we have seen, is a tedious, incremental process in which knowledge and skills are doled out in tiny pieces. It is neither a fun nor a profitable way to spend early childhood, but at least it is quite doable. Progress in early learning is measured in a binary format—plus or minus—in which a minus indicates a deficit that needs working on. In counting, for example, a child who can count to three earns a plus on that particular item but still has a minus on the next sequential step, counting to five. Fortunately, in preschool, counting, like all early learning, is a finite achievement (counting to twenty is the gold standard). Likewise, there are only twenty-six letters to learn, only eight crayons in the box, so by the time the child enters kindergarten, almost every early learning objective on the child's individual assessment has been moved from the minus to the plus column.

Unfortunately, developmental milestones are also recorded in the same binary format in which minuses are considered deficits to be worked on, an approach to child development that seems to willfully disregard fundamental principles of child development.

This much we know is true:

- Development occurs in a predetermined sequence. We cannot change the order in which it happens. An infant will roll over before she sits up; sit up before she stands up.
- Developmental milestones may occur earlier and later in each individual child than is typically expected. One child may get her first tooth at four months, another child not until eight months.
- There is little we can do to speed up the achievement of developmental milestones. The tooth will come when it is good and ready.

- There is absolutely no advantage to the child if the developmental milestone occurs earlier or later. The child who waits for the first tooth until eight months will have just as healthy teeth and just as pretty a smile as the child who gets the tooth at four months. The child who does not walk until sixteen months will eventually be just as physically competent as the child who walks at ten months.
- Typical development requires typical experiences. There is a window of opportunity during early childhood in which these experiences must occur. Otherwise certain milestones may never be achieved at all.

Consider three six-year-old children on their first day of baseball practice. Their moms watch in various states of anxiety from the bleachers. The first child's mom is anxious. She has been determined since her child's birth that when the appointed day arrived, her child would be baseball ready. She and her son have been playing with balls, rolling balls, bouncing balls, and tossing balls since the day he was born. She has been teaching him the rules of baseball for as long as he can remember.

The second child's mom is much less anxious. She has provided her child with all sorts of typical experiences, including ball playing, but has not had any particular agenda. The child expressed a desire to play peewee baseball, so here they are.

The third mom is thrilled to be there and is perhaps a bit anxious. Her child is a walking miracle. He was born blind, but at age five and a half, he had surgery that restored his eyesight. She hopes he is ready for baseball.

The three children stand side by side, waiting for the coach to throw them a baseball. As the ball hurtles toward child number one, six years of baseball readiness training kick in. He raises his glove in front of his face, and the ball comes to an abrupt halt squarely in the webbing of his glove.

As the ball hurtles toward child number two, six years of typical sensory experiences and typical development kick in. She raises her glove in front of her face, and the ball comes to an abrupt halt squarely in the webbing of her glove.

As the ball hurtles toward child number three, five years of sensory deprivation and atypical development kick in. He raises his glove six inches to the left of his face, and the ball comes to an abrupt halt squarely on his unprotected nose.

For child number two, typical experiences created the pathways in her brain that provided her with the depth perception and the hand-eye coordination necessary to catch the ball. She might not be as prepared to play baseball as child number one—maybe when she hits the ball she'll run to third base. On the other hand, if she bats second or third, she will observe which way other children run, and she'll know what to do. It's not rocket science. She may become an even more successful baseball player than child number one, depending on their respective natural abilities.

Child number three, however, may have been born with greater potential than either of the other two, but sensory deprivation during his critical early years did not allow development of the pathways that served child number two so well. With intense physical therapy and lots of practice, he may yet learn to catch a ball, but the odds of him ever becoming a great baseball player are very long.

When the ball is thrown to child number three, he is developmentally unprepared for the task at hand, and he suffers the consequences. But what if, in a misguided desire to help their children achieve baseball readiness, the parents of number one and two had tried to speed up the natural maturation process and had started throwing fastballs right at their children's noses at an age when they were also developmentally unprepared—perhaps only four years old? Would baseball readiness be the result? No. The result would be bloody noses and children who hate baseball.

Throwing Too Many Fastballs in the Quest for School Readiness

Yet throwing a fastball at children too young to catch it is an every-day consequence of school readiness goals and data gathering. The system is designed so that any objective not yet achieved, whether it be early learning or child development, is by definition a deficit, and teachers will continue to try to turn minuses into pluses even though no amount of teaching can make the developmental objective occur. In a best case scenario, the outcome is merely comical. An infant/toddler program might not actually require teachers to work on the objective "The child will get his first tooth," but without the slightest hint of irony, will in fact expect teachers to work on developmental goals such as "The child will roll over," "The child will sit up," "The child will crawl," and "The child will pull up"—developmental milestones that the child will master whether or not the objective is identified as a goal, written in a lesson plan, or entered in a database. In fact, all of these milestones will be achieved even if the child never attends an early childhood program.

It would all be pretty funny if it were not for the fact that not all developmental goals are written for babies, nor are they confined to physical development. A great many of them also address emotional development, social development, and cognitive development that, like physical development, occur through maturity and cannot be hurried along any more than the first tooth.

What we have here is yet another extraordinary disconnect between what we know and what we do. We understand in theory that the developmental chasm between the four-year-old and five-year-old is deep and wide and cannot be crossed simply by writing lesson plans and objectives that try to will children into maturity, but we act as if all preschool programs have no value to children other than providing a dress rehearsal for real school. Once schools got into the business of preschool and Head Start capitulated to the accountability model, both systems have acted as if the best way to prepare a child for the experience of kindergarten is to enroll children in preschool classrooms that mimic kindergarten as closely as possible. (Not such a bad idea if it were the children's garden that was imitated, rather than the modern version that itself aspires to be first grade.)

In fairness, policy makers at the state and federal level would take very strong exception to this characterization of early childhood education. All of their programs, they would point out, are instructed to provide services that are developmentally appropriate. But it is a mixed message indeed when these same programs are instructed to use assessments that identify unmet developmental goals as deficits and when these same programs are required to demonstrate progress in achieving those goals.

It is true that to be successful in kindergarten a five-year-old must be able to sit quietly in a group and pay attention to the teacher, but school readiness goals would have the four-year-old doing the same thing: If a five-year-old needs to be able to follow directions and stay on task, then a four-year-old must also. If a five-year-old must be able to share, take turns, resolve conflicts, and express emotions appropriately, then a four-year-old must also. And even though early childhood professionals understand completely that the rate of development varies widely among children, there is very little allowance made for children whose development lags behind.

To see how these beliefs play out in practice for children, let's consider the story of Twanna, a child who is so spectacularly unsuccessful in preschool that her parents take her out of the program, but who nevertheless, through the ordinary process of maturity, succeeds quite well in kindergarten. Let's see what also happens to some of her classmates who do not achieve critical developmental milestones as quickly as these programs require and who find themselves directly in the path of the rapidly approaching baseball.

Twanna's Story: It's All about Maturity

A five-year-old girl, Twanna, begins her first day of kindergarten that, except for a brief and unsuccessful two-week stint in preschool, is her first formal encounter with the educational system. She has spent most of her early childhood at home with her mom and her two siblings. Upon entering her kindergarten classroom, an adult she has never met before in her life tells her to sit down at her desk. She has no experience sitting down at desks, but what does she do? She sits down at her desk next to Warren, a boy she knows who lives in her building. Then the teacher says, "Class" (no one had ever called her "Class" before), "I need you to look up here at the board." What does she do? She looks at the board. The teacher then proceeds to teach this morning's lesson—simple addition—linearly and abstractly. The young student listens attentively, taking it all in.

It's a beautiful sunny day, though, and after a while her attention wanders to the playground right outside the window. The swing sure looks inviting. Nevertheless, she does not give in to the urge to leave her seat and head for the swing. The swing, however, makes her think of her walks to her neighborhood playground with her mama. As her attention wanders further from her teacher, something about the teacher's tone brings her back, and she realizes the teacher is handing out lined paper on which the students are to print their names. She prints her name. Warren does the same thing.

The morning goes by slowly. The tedium of sitting at the desk is relieved by the opportunity to go to reading group in the back of the classroom. Twanna participates when prompted, correctly identifying alphabet letters in the alphabet book and joining the group in affirming that the letter *m* makes the *mmmm* sound.

Finally, at 11:30 the moment of truth arrives—the holy grail of school readiness.

The teacher asks the class to put their pencils away, slide their chairs under their desks, and line up at the door. It is time to go to the cafeteria. Although she has not spent two years in preschool rehearsing for this pivotal moment in her early education, Twanna nevertheless complies with the request. She responds correctly to the teacher's three-step instructions, but at the door Warren tries to push his way in front of her. She resists the urge to knock him flat and instead gives him the fierce glare that she uses when her big brother tries to commandeer the remote, and Warren quickly decides that the spot in line right behind Twanna will do just fine.

Twanna walks down the hall in absolute silence, as instructed by her teacher, marches into the cafeteria, sits at her table, and eats more or less silently, although the lunch monitor is also treated to one of her looks when he reminds her to observe the zero noise policy.

How is this child able to accomplish this series of amazing tasks without the benefit of preschool? How is she able to perform on equal footing with the other children in her class, almost all of whom had attended either the preschool program down the hall or the Head Start program in her housing authority neighborhood? It's not such a big mystery. Twanna has mastered these kindergarten readiness tasks the same way she has mastered tasks such as sitting up, crawling, walking, and talking. Like the developmental milestones of her infancy, almost all of these school readiness behaviors Twanna displays that morning were acquired naturally as she matured.

"What sound does the letter *m* make?" the teacher had asked. That was an easy one. Unlike most of his twenty-five cousins, the letter *m* is a model of consistency. It makes the same sound in any combination of letters and in any position within a word. What sound does the letter *m* make? Muh. Muh, Muh. Mother. *M* makes the *mmmm* sound. Easy enough from the point of view of most five-year-olds.

Twanna's thinking has matured enough that she grasps the concept that letters make sounds. Had someone attempted to teach her that same lesson even six months earlier, she would have become easily bored and distracted and would no doubt have found herself in trouble. Twanna's cognitive ability to understand the abstract idea that *m* makes a sound helps keep her engaged with the lesson. She is able to accomplish other developmental tasks as well, including to stay on task during the phonics lesson and to participate appropriately in the group, both of which are social-emotional developmental milestones identified in school readiness standards.

But what if she had not been able to successfully process the phonics lesson? What if Twanna had tried to learn that same lesson at age four?

Print a big capital letter *M* on a blank sheet of paper. Turn off the television and tell everyone in the house to be quiet. Hold the *M* up to your ear. Listen very hard. What sound is it making? No matter how hard or how long you listen, good old *M* is not ever going to make a sound. Trains make sounds. Birds make sounds.

Alphabet letters, on the other hand, represent sounds. When strung together, alphabet letters also represent words.

Quite a conceptual leap for the young child. Like the developmental tasks of her infancy—sitting up and rolling over—understanding that letters represent sounds requires that the child achieve a certain degree of cognitive maturity before achieving mastery, as evidenced by one of Twanna's earlier encounters with phonics. When she was four years old, Twanna's brother came home from first grade eager to teach school to his little sister. The lesson that day was the letter *d*.

"What letter does *dog* start with?" he asked his captive student.

She looked at him blankly. He gave her a hint, "Duh, duh, duh dog," he intoned. "What letter makes the *duh* sound?"

A happy expression of comprehension spread across her features. The lightbulb had gone off. "Duh, duh, duh double you!" she exclaimed.

"Wanna play go fish?" her brother asked.

"Sure," she agreed. "School is boring."

But at age five, Twanna is able to deal with phonics and addition as well as other abstract tasks, such as being physically in one place (at her desk) while imagining she is somewhere else (the playground). The developmental ability to be in one place physically and another mentally is not taught or learned, but it is an essential developmental skill that enables most people age five and over to successfully complete any number of tasks, including the ability to get through school, to attend seminars and training sessions, and to sit through church.

Another essential skill that Twanna has mastered that comes with maturity is the ability to control her impulses. (In early childhood education, we like to say that she has developed the executive function—the cognitive mechanism that creates the necessary space between emotion and response that allows the child to choose an alternate action other than the one guided by pure emotion.) It is an ability for Twanna that is still developing, but it has reached the point that she can navigate the demands of school. She does not try to leave her seat and walk out the door in order to play on the swing. She does not knock Warren flat on his back when he tries to get in front of her in line. She remains reasonably quiet in the hallway and the cafeteria.

When Twanna was two years old, that level of self-control and intellectual development was not even on the radar screen. On Daddy's weekend, when he took her to the giant discount store to buy some milk and cat food, he made the mistake of letting her walk beside him as he maneuvered his cart down the pet food aisle. She was next seen again thirty very anxious moments later when security finally found her hiding in the middle of the junior miss dress rack.

It was a long time before Mama ever let Daddy forget that one. When accompanying her mother to the store, no amount of pleading ever earned Twanna a release from the shopping cart child seat. These days, however, big grown-up kindergarten student that she has become, Twanna finally gets to walk next to the cart (although now she would rather ride), and it never even crosses her mind to run or to hide. Instead, she stays right next to her mother, begging her for every single toy and every sugary treat that has ever appeared on her television screen.

What's the difference between two-year-old Twanna and five-year-old Twanna? The development of her executive function skills.

Not all of the children in Twanna's kindergarten class are as far along in their development as she is. A few of the boys, Tyrone, Marcus, and Warren, are still very impulsive and easily distracted.

Like Twanna a year earlier, these kindergarten children still respond to frustration by hitting and throwing things. They are still very much hands-on learners and cannot yet process information such as simple addition and phonics simply by sitting and listening to the teacher. They disrupt group time and tend to be constantly in trouble. Warren attended the Head Start program in his neighborhood, but Tyrone and Marcus attended preschool right down the hall and arrived in kindergarten with well-established reputations. They were, according to their preschool teacher, "aggressive" and "defiant." Because their emotional and intellectual development has not yet caught up to the demands of school, these two boys will struggle in kindergarten and remain in trouble for the rest of their unhappy tenure in the school system. Twanna had come very close to meeting the same fate. She was enrolled in the same Head Start program as Warren at age four.

Like most preschool classrooms, it was a classroom designed intentionally to imitate kindergarten, even though many children like Twanna were not nearly mature enough to handle it. The program meant well. It was trying to prepare children for school, even though such preparation would involve having Twanna and her classmates develop faster than their DNA would allow. On Twanna's first morning at Head Start, her teacher, an adult whom she had never seen before in her life, told her to sit quietly in the circle with the other children, legs crossed, hands in her lap, and to listen to her teacher. She tried, but developmentally, she was not able to process the rote learning about days of the week that passed for a group lesson that morning. Her attention soon wandered to all the cool stuff displayed on shelves throughout the room. When she spotted the playdough, she jumped up from the circle without a second thought and headed straight for the shelf. (As with many children her age, when the mind wanders, the feet follow.) She did not just leave her teacher mentally, she left him physically, and she became very annoyed and resentful when he admonished her.

"It's not time for that now, Twanna," he reminded her. "Come back here and sit with your friends."

Unlike five-year-old Twanna, whose response to the lunch monitor was to be simultaneously obedient in behavior but defiant in demeanor, four-year-old Twanna lacked the maturity to make a good decision when given a direct command. It didn't help that she had inherited quite a stubborn streak from her mother. With the can of playdough held in a vise grip in her hands, her feet planted wide apart and arms folded across her chest, Twanna stood her ground. The assistant teacher had to carry Twanna back to the circle and hold her in place.

Later in the day, when her "friend" Warren took her favorite car away from her, she knocked him flat on his bottom. He wailed. Her teacher intervened immediately, comforting Warren and then providing Twanna with a lesson in conflict resolution.

"That hurt Warren," he explained to her. "Aren't you sorry that you made him cry? Don't you want to apologize?"

She was not and she did not.

"He took my car!"

"Well, then, don't hit him. Tell him how you feel."

This time Twanna did comply.

Treating Warren to the most contemptuous look she could muster, Twanna looked him right in the eye and shouted, "*How I feel, Warren!*" right into his face and then stomped away.

When the time came to sit down with Twanna's mother to discuss Twanna's progress toward accomplishing school readiness goals, Twanna's teacher would find it very difficult to put a positive spin on it. Her individual assessment revealed more deficits than the federal budget, and among her many minuses were the unhappy observations that she was not able to stay on task for even one minute, let alone ten minutes as expected by year's end. She was unable to follow a simple one-step direction, much less a three-step direction. Twanna was unable to share, would not display empathy or sympathy, and did not participate cooperatively in groups. Based on these and other developmental deficits, Twanna was not meeting widely held expectations. Would the mother be willing to sign a permission slip to have Twanna evaluated so that Twanna might receive some professional help?

Her mother would not. Much to Twanna's relief, her mom took her out of the program.

At age four, her classmate Warren was no better suited for school than Twanna. Although prone to impulsiveness for reasons of temperament and learning style, he did not draw nearly the negative attention that other children, including Twanna, managed to bring on themselves. Warren, for example, was as disengaged during group time as was Twanna. But when the teacher was doing yet another repetitive lesson on the days of the week or the weather, he did not usually wander. Instead, he would fidget, sometimes lying on his back with his feet straight up in the air, pumping an imaginary upside-down bicycle. Every once in a while he would crawl like a bug over to the blocks, but unlike Twanna, he returned meekly to the circle once reprimanded by the teacher. When a story was read in group, he did not sit quietly on his spot, but instead moved closer to the teacher, commando style on his belly so he could get a better look at the pictures—a behavior tolerated most of the time by the adults in the room.

Nor was Warren any better than Twanna at negotiating conflict with his peers or in displaying empathy. In fact, it was Warren who often instigated conflict by taking toys from his classmates. Most of the time if that behavior caught the attention of his teachers, it quickly became one of those pointless "Who had it first?" investigations that always ended with the admonishment that the children share. If another child hit him, pushed him, or took something from him, Warren would not "use his words" but would howl until the teacher intervened. It was annoying, but howling and whining did not raise the same red flags as behaviors such as knocking people down and hitting displayed by Twanna in her Head Start classroom or Marcus and Tyrone in their preschool classroom, even though all of these behaviors were manifestations of the same kind of emotional and cognitive immaturity.

Twanna's teacher did not approach Twanna's mother lightly about the possibility that her child might need professional help. He and his assistant had discussed the child's behavior with each other at length, and they had consulted with their superiors before making such a suggestion. (A specified number of minuses on the assessment instrument triggers an automatic in-house referral.)

"Have you tried being more flexible with Twanna?" they were asked by their supervisor. "Maybe it would be all right if she was able to play with playdough while you led the circle time. Maybe she doesn't always have to come to the small-group activities. Maybe she just needs more choices?"

"No," the teachers responded as one. "Her kindergarten teacher is not going to let Twanna just hang out and do whatever she feels like. It's important that we teach her how to behave in school while we have a chance."

"Ah yes," the supervisor thought to herself. "I've heard this one before. If her kindergarten teacher is going to make her miserable next year, we better make her miserable now so that she can get used to it."

The supervisor has learned by now that the practices of her teachers are very entrenched, and there is not much she can do about it. She could consider sending them to another training, for all the good that will do, but it is her experience that the belief systems and paradigms of individual preschool classroom teachers will always trump training as well as anything she has to suggest about how best to support young children, even though her advice is based on sound principles of child development.

"Go ahead and see what her parents have to say," she tells them wearily.

But if poor practices are purely the fault of teachers, doesn't anybody wonder why so many teachers engage in them? Was it the teachers' idea to spend their day trying to "work on" developmental milestones? Did they invent school readiness standards and performance objectives that penalize children for not developing fast enough? If given the opportunity, wouldn't they much rather just relax and enjoy the children, spending their time doing cool things, playing, and talking?

What this supervisor, as well as policy makers far above her in the food chain, fails to acknowledge is the impact of public policy on classroom practice. If administrators and decision makers really do not want teachers penalizing a child because her first tooth has not yet arrived, they would not issue developmental performance objectives in the first place, nor would they make teachers accountable for the child's progress. From the perspective of the teacher, developmental objectives such as "Stays on task for one minute" and "Participates cooperatively in group" are no different from an early learning objective such as counting to ten. They will all appear on lesson plans and all will be entered into the electronic database. The teacher's effectiveness will be assessed by his children's progress on all performance objectives, be they early learning or child development.

And what are the consequences for children like Twanna, Tyrone, and Marcus when the teachers constantly make demands on them for which they are developmentally unprepared?

A fast ball, right in the nose, every single time.

If Twanna had stayed in her early childhood program, her developmental arc would have been identical to that if she had not attended any kind of program at all. The only difference would be that if she had remained in that program, by the time she arrived in kindergarten she would be labeled as a behavior problem and would hate school.

Assessing Social-Emotional Development

Of Twanna's many deficits, those most troubling to her teachers were her poor social skills. But early childhood classrooms are often not the ideal setting for children to acquire these skills, and not just because of unrealistic expectations. Just as she acquired language, Twanna gains social skills by observing how adults behave in a wide variety of contexts. She sees her parents when they are getting along and when they are mad at each other—how Mom expresses her anger when Daddy is late picking Twanna up for weekend visits and how she shows appreciation when he keeps Twanna for an unscheduled weekend when Twanna's mother has to work overtime. She sees how her parents treat their friends and how they treat people they don't like, how they interact with strangers and how they interact with people they know—how her daddy is patient with the clerk at the fast-food restaurant when she gets his order wrong but yells ugly words at drivers who cut him off. She listens while her mother has angry confrontations with bill collectors on the telephone and watches when her mother gives the homeless person on the corner the last dollar in her purse.

Twanna listens to her mother and her grandmother when they talk badly about the lady across the hall, and she sees how they rush to assist her when she slips on the ice on the front steps. Twanna observes acts of kindness and acts of selfishness. She sees adults in their everyday lives when they are patient and when they are annoyed. She agrees solemnly when her mother tells her never to tell a lie, and she is not at all surprised when her mother calls in sick when she is feeling just fine. Twanna learns how to deal with her older brother when he tries to boss her around, and she learns how to help her mother take care of the baby.

Social development is very much like language development in that there is never a particular experience or specific lesson that teaches the child to perform as desired, nor an identifiable moment of mastery, but rather an ongoing development of behaviors learned in the context of everyday experiences. A child who experiences respect in his daily interactions with caregivers and parents will learn to treat others the same way, as will the child who experiences empathy and sympathy. Likewise, the child who experiences fairness will learn to treat others fairly.

All of this social learning occurs gradually, organically, and unconsciously, and like language, can best be observed in unscripted settings. A three-year-old sees a playmate in distress and gives her a toy (only to snatch it away thirty seconds later). A one-year-old pushes a fellow toddler down onto the seat of her pants because she is in her way and then gives the crying child a hug. There is never a precise moment in time in which the minus becomes a plus. However unpredictable, messy, and sometimes even chaotic it may be, the daily field trip to the laboratory of real life is how all human beings acquire social skills.

The daily field trip to the laboratory of real life is how all human beings acquire social skills.

When Twanna's teachers say that her social skills are lacking, what they really mean is that those skills cannot be accurately measured using the reductionist methodology provided to them.

If the executive function is her first tooth, it has not yet become readily observable. It is still below the gum line, arriving later for Twanna than it did for the child sitting next to her, but emerging nevertheless. And *empathy*, the root of social behaviors like sharing and taking turns, is still hanging around waiting for intellectual development to catch up. Twanna has experienced empathy at home, but to actually feel empathy, Twanna must be able to understand how someone else feels, to be able to grasp what it is like to be in someone else's shoes—quite an intellectual leap for a four-year-old. The teacher is absolutely right to tell Twanna that it hurts Warren's feelings when he is pushed down, but those words have little meaning to Twanna just yet. Twanna is still very much engaged in the primary social-emotional developmental task of all preschool children.

She is still trying to figure out who is in *her* shoes.

How does she feel? She'll let us know just as soon as she finds out.

Labeling the "Bad Boys"

Gather our hundred teachers back together again and ask them to name a child in their care who has been a behavior problem. There will be many to choose from, so ask them to picture that child who they pray every morning will not get off the bus. Ask them to write the child's name down on a piece of paper. Then ask them to stand up if they wrote down the name of . . . a boy.

Ninety embarrassed early childhood professionals will stand (including those who identified Tyrone and Marcus) and will become even more embarrassed when they see how many of their colleagues are standing with them. There has been much written about why early childhood programs label boys as failures at earlier and earlier ages. (Kind of the opposite of school readiness, isn't it?) But in the context of school readiness goals, one of the many possible answers just leaps out.

Boys mature more slowly than girls. (Many preschool teachers reading this book probably have a man at home who they hope will grow up some day. Don't hold your breath.)

As long as developmental milestones are reduced to performance objectives and treated as deficits to be corrected, school readiness programs will continue to fail children who are developing more slowly. They will consequently fail boys at a higher rate than girls.

Early Information vs. Early Experience

The discerning reader no doubt noticed that Twanna's successful debut in kindergarten was not entirely a matter of maturity. There was a significant amount of early learning that had taken place as well. She could identify alphabet letters and print her name. She seemed to understand what was meant when the teacher said,

"Line up at the door." She was familiar enough with numbers that she could follow the lesson on simple addition.

Doesn't a child have to attend preschool to know these things?

Not necessarily. Twanna did not grow up on another planet, so the concept of waiting in line was not unfamiliar to her. She had spent time in grocery stores and fast-food restaurants. Even a child who somehow missed those experiences but still had the prerequisite developmental skills would successfully line up once she observed the other children doing it. Like the learning that occurred when the young baseball player watched his teammates run to first base, it is not rocket science—hardly worth the amount of time and effort devoted to it in preschool.

As for the rest of the early learning Twanna displayed, it was her parents who taught her. Neither of them had studied child development, so their definition of school readiness was a narrow academic one. Daddy set aside an hour of every weekend visit for her to practice printing her name on lined paper. Both parents drilled her on the alphabet. They practiced counting to twenty and they taught her to recognize numerals, although they referred to them as numbers.

Oddly enough, the preschool teachers who had attempted to prepare Warren and Marcus and Tyrone for school success *had* studied child development, but nevertheless believed in much the same definition of school readiness as Twanna's parents, as did the early childhood programs that employed them. In fact, almost every child in Twanna's kindergarten class had attended an early childhood program, and almost every one of them had begun school with the same set of knowledge and skills as Twanna.

But doesn't Twanna's story prove that they are right? It's all very fine to talk about language experiences and social development, but there is a bottom line of knowledge that the child needs in order to be prepared for kindergarten, and not every parent is going to provide it. Doesn't there need to be a list somewhere that tells everyone exactly what the child needs to know in order to be successful on that first day?

Okay. Here it is. This is what a child needs to know in order to be successful on the first day of kindergarten:

Almost nothing.

"Almost nothing" means that the kindergarten readiness checklist consists of only about two hundred pieces of information. These would include the eight colors in the crayon box; half a dozen shapes; seven days; twelve months; four seasons; twenty-six letters; twenty numerals; basic personal information, including first and last name, gender, address, and date of birth; opposites; simple analogies; food groups; the weather; some basic prepositions; comparative adjectives; author; illustrator; a few dinosaurs; means of transportation; community helpers; and a farm animal or two (general knowledge is a bit arbitrary).

Taken as a whole, the sum of kindergarten readiness constitutes only one percent of the total vocabulary a child would accrue through exposure to language-rich experiences. So afraid are preschool programs of the kindergarten checklist, though, that language-rich experiences that could be provided by adults in communication mode are sacrificed for the endless repetition of the same facts day in and day out by adults who never venture out of linear instructional mode. Expectations are so minimal, the bar set so low, we behave as if we were training chimpanzees to communicate by pointing to pictures rather than supporting human children in learning how to communicate with words.

Way too many children from low-income families grow up in homes where the majority of language is management talk.

Yet we persist in bringing children from those homes into early childhood classrooms at great expense so that they can spend their very precious early years jumping through hoops, hearing nothing but management talk, and engaging in "drive-by" interactions all day long.

And here is the sad part.

Because both their preschool classrooms and kindergartens substituted information for experience and thereby set the bar so low, neither Twanna nor Warren nor a disgraceful number of their classmates who were successful that first day of kindergarten will be successful in school. Because kindergarten readiness is measured by the child's knowledge of a few facts while school success is dependent on the child's ability to engage in complex communication, these children will fall further and further behind every year. They will learn how to decode print but will not know how to use it to express their thoughts and their experiences or how to comprehend the ideas and experiences of others.

Like the baseball player who had been deprived of sensory information during his first five years, Twanna and her classmates were deprived of rich language when they needed it most, and no amount of remedial education will ever allow them to reach the potential they were born with. By third grade, standardized testing will reveal an achievement gap between these children and their more affluent competitors that could easily have been predicted by the language gap identified at age three and even earlier.

Everyone knew it was there. No one did anything about it.

Chapter 4

———

Changing the Way We Talk to Young Children

The folks who run state pre-K programs and Head Start are very smart people who care deeply about children. Many of them serve the accountability model with no small amount of reluctance. Still, they would no doubt claim in defense of standards-driven early childhood education that language development and critical-thinking skills have not been abandoned but are explicitly included in early learning standards and in performance objectives that are intended to address the language gap that sets up Twanna, her friends, and way too many of the children of poverty for failure in school. Which is, of course, exactly what is wrong with early childhood education.

Consider this conversation between the parent of a three-year-old boy and her child's teacher.

"Mrs. Stokes," Scotty's teacher begins, looking up from her laptop, "Now that I've shared the results of our initial assessment of Scotty with you and we've identified some things we're working on, I wonder if you would mind sharing some of your goals for him as well. You are his first and best teacher, after all."

Scotty is enrolled in the school district's pre-K program for disadvantaged children, and his teacher is making the first of her semi-annual home visits to the two-bedroom housing authority apartment shared by Scotty, his mom, and his teenage sister (currently sprawled on the couch texting her friends with single-minded intensity).

Sitting across from the teacher at her kitchen table, Mrs. Stokes mulls over the question. "Yes, actually, I will," she replies. "I'm very concerned that Scotty hasn't learned his name yet." From her perch on the couch, the teenager snorts. Mom shoots her the "Just wait until this lady leaves" look, which the teenager actively ignores.

"Tell me what you mean," the teacher asks.

"Well, I ask him his name several times a day, and sometimes he tells me Scotty, but sometimes he doesn't answer at all. Am I doing the right thing by asking him this all the time?"

"Absolutely," Scotty's teacher nods her head vigorously. "In fact, the ability to state personal information like full name, address, and so on is a very important school readiness goal. I'll enter it into his individual database, and we'll work on it at school. Every day at morning meeting we have roll call where each child recites his personal information so that children will get used to doing it the way they do in kindergarten. We'll track his progress on the computer and let you know when he's achieved mastery."

Because her back is turned to the couch, Scotty's teacher doesn't see the teenager roll her eyes, but Mom does. Now it's her turn to ignore her daughter.

"You could do that for me?"

"Oh yes, our database tracks his progress on all of his goals. We'll send you progress reports every quarter, just like real school."

As soon as the teacher is out the door, Mrs. Stokes turns on her daughter. "I can't believe you behaved so rudely in front of Scotty's teacher."

"Well I can't believe you ask Scotty to tell you his name ten times a day, Mom, and now you've got *them* doing it at his school.

"They were going to do it anyway."

"Maybe so, but he's three, Mom; he's not brain damaged. I mean, do you ever think what it's like to be Scotty and have you bugging him all the time about his name? He's like, 'Oh, No! My feeble-minded mom can't remember my name! What else will she forget? What if she forgets to put her clothes on when she goes to the store? I hope she doesn't take me with her.'"

"Very funny."

"Or else he's thinking 'What's my name? Omigod! I *thought* it was Scotty. You mean it *isn't* Scotty? If it isn't Scotty, then I'm not answering any of your questions until you tell me what it really is.'"

"If it's such a ridiculous question, then why is it a school readiness goal? And why do they track it on the computer? And anyway, I want him to know his address, too. What if he gets lost, or God forbid, somebody snatches him?"

"You've got a point there, Mom. He could tell the kidnappers where to send the ransom note."

"So what do *you* think we should do, Miss Know-it-all?"

"I don't know—quit asking him questions all day long, I guess. He knows his name because we call him by his name. If you think his address is so important, well . . . whenever I write a letter to Daddy, Scotty likes to draw pictures and send them, too. He can help me address the envelope. He knows we live in one place and Daddy lives somewhere else. He'll see that an address means 'that's where you live,' and that everybody has one."

"Oh, so you're a certified teacher now. I'll tell you what. Come back home with a master's degree, and then we'll talk."

"Whatever."

Talking to Children Like People

The untrained teenage sister understands intuitively what early childhood professionals—those who teach as well as those who write the standards that guide the teaching—seem to have forgotten. Children learn best through authentic interactions with adults and through meaningful experiences with the real world. Rather than learn to recite random information in hopes that it can someday be useful (to assist a kidnapper, for example), children use information in the real world

Children learn best through authentic interactions with adults and through meaningful experiences with the real world.

(address a letter to Daddy) and thereby learn not only the information but also how it is used and why it is important.

What the older sister is suggesting to her mother is that Scotty would be much better off if she simply learned to talk to him like a person. It is a skill that many parents seem to be born with. They converse with their children effortlessly and unconsciously throughout the day, although they might not be aware of the benefit to the child. On the other hand, perhaps they are. Listen to children on a playground, at a fast-food restaurant, or in a doctor's office. It's pretty obvious which ones are spoken to like people and which ones are not.

We can forgive Scotty's mom if she does not speak to Scotty like a person. Conversing with children does not come easily to her, and her interactions with Scotty are driven by her anxiety that Scotty might not learn everything he needs to know or learn how to behave in ways that are acceptable. Most of her interactions with him consist of either management talk ("Stop that!" "Put that away!") or pop quizzes about his name, colors, letters, and numbers.

Early childhood professionals, though, seem equally ill at ease talking to children, and the content of their interactions vary little from that of Scotty's mother in that it is also driven by anxiety that the child will not learn enough. In fact, if the leadership of Head Start and state preschool systems were able to spend time in actual classrooms, they would discover immediately that the logical and completely predictable response of preschool teachers to accountability and data gathering is identical to the response of every third-grade teacher in America since the dawn of the second Bush administration.

They teach to the test.

In so doing they remain in linear instructional mode almost exclusively and almost never venture into communication mode. The problem with the accountability model is that it represents a completely different *way of being* with children. Driven by performance objectives, teachers view children not as people with whom they are building relationships, but as walking, talking sets of deficits that need fixing. As a result, most interactions between teacher and child become bereft of any authentic human quality and take on instead a stilted, ritualized quality that is unique to the world of early childhood education.

To appreciate how artificial and contrived many teacher-child interactions are, consider the interactions of two total strangers seated side by side on a nonstop flight from Nashville to Tampa. During the ninety-minute flight, they will take turns sharing so much information—families, jobs, hometowns, life histories, political and religious views, and personal philosophies—that the poor passenger in the row in front of them will be begging the crew to divert the flight to Atlanta so she doesn't have to listen to one more anecdote.

The interactions between the two passengers is a condensed, transparent, easily observable, stripped-down version of how neighbors, classmates, and coworkers get to know each other over time and develop relationships of mutual respect and trust. But wouldn't it be strange indeed if those same two passengers found themselves sitting next to each other on the return flight (the passenger in the row in front of them took no chances—she rented a car) and acted as if they had never seen each other in their lives and asked all the same questions and gave all the same replies? It would be stranger still if only one of the two passengers had asked questions of his companion but had not shared even a little bit about himself while the second passenger had answered every question but had shown zero interest in his companion.

That would be an early childhood classroom.

Like Scotty's mother, teachers ask children every day to recite the same list of personal information as well as the rest of the kindergarten teachers' checklist, as if the teachers were suffering from the onset of dementia and could not remember a thing. And although they spend all day every day asking children questions, they never reciprocate by sharing any information about themselves. Teachers are often amused at children they encounter at a grocery store who are befuddled by their teacher's appearance in a setting outside the classroom. "They think we live here at the school," the teachers tell one another, shaking their heads. None of them considers the possibility that the child is so confused because teachers act as if they live there.

Two teachers, Mr. Brown and Ms. White, provide a Halloween activity for their children. The performance objective is to identify facial features, although, naturally, colors and shapes are part of the lesson as well. Eight children gather at each of two tables to draw faces on orange construction paper pumpkins. "These are pumpkins," Mr. Brown informs the group. "Do any of you have a pumpkin at your house for Halloween? What color is the pumpkin?" All eight children respond with such enthusiasm and with answers so completely random that Mr. Brown is obliged to shush them. "It's orange," he announces. "Can you say, 'orange'?"

The children can.

Mr. Brown proceeds to draw features on his pumpkin, quizzing the children as he goes. "What's this?" he asks. "What's this?" One of the children shouts immediately, "It's a pumpkin!"

"Yes, but what part of the pumpkin?"

Doubt and uncertainty cloud the children's faces. Evidently, they didn't know a construction paper pumpkin had parts.

"It's his smile," he explains.

"His smile," they intone. His nose and his eyes quickly follow, and soon the children are drawing faces on their own construction paper pumpkins.

"I have my mama's smile," a little girl, Consuela, remarks.

"You have your mama's smile? That's nice," Mr. Brown responds. "And what body part is this?" he asks, pointing to the nose. Personal information is not one of the performance objectives of this lesson, and even if it were, Mr. Brown might not recognize information concerning the origin of Consuela's smile as relevant.

Although Mr. Brown is locked into teaching his performance objectives, Ms. White sees an opportunity for a teachable moment.

"Your mother smiles because she's happy," Ms. White points out. "What does she do when she's sad?"

Consuela pauses a moment to consider the question. It is an open-ended question intended to make Consuela think about her response, and it has the intended effect.

"My mother isn't sad," Consuela responds.

"Everyone is sad sometimes," Ms. White assures her. "When people are sad, they *frown*. They make a sad face, like Ms. White does when children don't play nice." (Ms. White often lapses into her odd habit of referring to herself in the third person whenever she addresses children.)

The activity continues, as does the interview. As individual children complete the pumpkin face, they are asked to identify the facial features as well as reaffirm the color and shape. The last child to finish his pumpkin answers the same set of questions as the first child, as if he had just shown up for the lesson instead of sitting at the same table with all the others the entire time.

By the end of the activity, the wall knows what color the pumpkins are.

The Power of Normal Human Discourse

To fully appreciate how bizarre this behavior is and how standards-driven education negatively impacts the building of relationships and community in a classroom, one need look no further than the normal human conversation between Ms. White and Mr. Brown in the break room before the children arrived.

That very morning, over a cup of coffee, Ms. White had told Mr. Brown a story about yelling at her daughter because she had received detention for tardiness. "I shouldn't have raised my voice," she admitted. "I guess I've got my daddy's temper."

Mr. Brown did not respond by saying, "You've got your daddy's temper? That's nice. What color is your coffee?" Instead, he had replied instantly that when he was growing up, his mother had always attributed any and all of his undesirable qualities to his absent father. Ms. White, in turn, did not respond by asking, "What letter does coffee start with?" but had instead rejoined with a story about how her own stepfather had been such a blessing to her family and had loved all her mom's children as if they were his own.

In normal human discourse, in communication mode, it appears that people respond contingently to the stories of others. They share their feelings, their ideas, and their experiences with little or no prompting, and quite often without a great deal of forethought. Both Mr. Brown and Ms. White assume that the other party is interested in their story and that the response to the sharing will be respectful. When Ms. White reveals something about herself, Mr. Brown feels more comfortable about reciprocating, and trust between them continues to grow. Each small sharing becomes another small piece of the ongoing process of building a relationship.

When Consuela shares personal information about herself, though, the response of both adults is quite different. By replying "That's nice" and continuing with his lesson, Mr. Brown demonstrates to Consuela, during this exchange and in others throughout the day, that his main concern is not relationship building or communicating, it is to complete the task at hand. And in this classroom, like most classrooms, there is always a task at hand. The result is that the language Consuela and her classmates hear consists mostly of management talk that differs very little from the management talk they hear at home.

Ms. White is somewhat more respectful than Mr. Brown in that she tries to create a teachable moment out of Consuela's comment. From her point of view, her input is exactly what she has been taught to do. She is teaching Consuela a concept in the context of what is important to Consuela in the moment—her mother's smile as opposed to construction paper pumpkins. It simply would not occur to her to respond to Consuela's remark by sharing a story about herself, the way she responded to Mr. Brown earlier in the day. Her view of Consuela is that this is a student who needs to be taught lessons. The teachable moment is just an alternate vehicle for delivering that lesson.

Teachers and parents teach seven days a week, twenty-four hours a day, whether they know it or not.

Ms. White does not understand that there is really no such thing as *a* teachable moment. Because children learn from every experience and from every interaction, every moment is teachable. During early childhood, teachers and parents teach seven days a week, twenty-four hours a day, whether they know it or not, whether they intend to or not, or whether they are prepared to do so or not.

Consuela already knew what is meant by eyes, ears, nose, and mouth. What she learns from *this* lesson is that nobody cares that she has her mother's smile.

This is not to say that Consuela does not have a positive relationship with her teachers. She does. She loves them, in fact. They take care of her. They're nice to her. They love her, too. But they do not take her seriously as a person. If Ms. White had been sitting on that airplane and her fellow passenger had remarked, "I have my mother's smile," Ms. White might have said something diplomatic like, "She must be a very attractive woman." Her companion might have replied, "Would you like to see her picture?" and out would come the smartphone. Ms. White would have displayed polite interest and might have reciprocated with photos from her own smartphone.

When Consuela says, "I have my mother's smile," she summons forth a pivotal moment. She has revealed a piece of personal information, and now each teacher must decide whether he or she is there to support language and emotional development or to teach school, to provide crucial early experiences or to master performance objectives, to treat Consuela with the same respect and dignity as they would a stranger on an airplane, or to treat her like an empty spreadsheet awaiting data entry.

Let us rewind to that decisive moment and write an alternate ending.

"If you have your mother's smile, then she must be very beautiful, indeed," exclaims Ms. White. "Let's see if there's a picture of her in our family photos."

Ms. White retrieves the classroom family photo album, and together she and the other children examine every photograph. Ms. White does not confine herself to pointing out family resemblances, facial features, and expressions but instead makes comments about every picture. Some remind her of her own family and her own childhood, and she tells whatever stories come to mind, as do the children. Some children feel left out, though, because their parents never sent in their family photos, so Ms. White helps them look on the Internet to see if their mothers have photos on Facebook.

Of course, many programs would not approve of any kind of deviation from the daily agenda, and many more would be aghast at the thought of encouraging children to use something as open-ended and dangerous as the Internet in a classroom. But even teachers who work under such anxiety-driven constraints can still decide to talk and act like human beings. For example, when Ms. White hits a dead end by asking Consuela, "What does your mother do when she is sad?" Mr. Brown could come to the rescue with a contingent response—the way actual people do when they talk.

"How about you, Ms. White? What do you do when you're feeling a little bit unhappy?"

"Do you promise not to make me feel like a complete fool?" (Because she's speaking to a person and not a child, Ms. White uses the correct personal pronoun and drops the affect of referring to herself in the third person.)

"I suppose so. Is it that embarrassing?"

"Yes it is. I find a romantic comedy on Netflix and eat a whole quart of cookie dough ice cream all by myself sitting on my sofa."

"Wow. A whole quart? That must cost you a lot of extra miles on the treadmill!"

"Isn't that how it always goes? You have to punish yourself just to reward yourself. What do *you* do when you're sad, Mr. Brown?"

"Well, I have a pretty sunny disposition, but if I do get kind of sad, I play basketball with my kids on my driveway."

"Yeah. I knew you would say something uplifting and I would feel like an idiot."

Without being asked, the children chime in with stories about ice cream, Netflix, and basketball, as well as several other responses that seem completely random, until the teachers ask questions that reveal a connection to something else that was said. Consuela, who had responded minimally to the original question, "What does your mother do when she is sad?" informs everyone that she had strawberry ice cream for her birthday and that her baby cousin spilled it all over her brand-new birthday dress (we're uncertain as to whether that made her mother frown or smile), which sets off an avalanche of birthday stories.

By taking children seriously and venturing ever so briefly into communication mode, Ms. White and Mr. Brown have successfully prompted the children to communicate their experiences with words. Better yet, their short conversation with each other resembles very closely the conversations that the children of well-educated professionals hear all the time—the kind of discourse that spurs brain development and gives those more privileged children such a competitive edge over other children upon entry into school.

Wait a minute. Ms. Smith and Mr. Brown *are* well-educated professionals. One of the very best tools at their disposal to support school readiness (second only to helping parents provide rich language modeling in their homes) would be simply to act like themselves throughout the day—to weave conversations with children *and with each other* into every nook and corner of the daily classroom routine. They could call it a language-rich classroom.

It would be a completely different way of being with children.

Notice that unlike many parents who talk about absolutely everything in front of their children in the mistaken belief that children are not paying any attention, Ms. White and Mr. Brown are keenly aware that the children under their care are always tuned in. Therefore, they deliberately filter their daily discourse to avoid inappropriate content. They keep it real—they do not filter out adult vocabulary and sentence structure, and they respect the ability of children to acquire language by hearing it used in context. They continue to address each other as intelligent adults and make no effort to dumb it down. But Ms. White does not say, "I've been a basket case ever since my divorce." And Mr. Brown avoids saying, "When I'm feeling really low, I head straight to the liquor store," although either or both of those statements may actually be true.

But these omissions are of little consequence. These two adults have entire lifetimes of appropriate experiences, ideas, stories, and feelings to share with each other and with children at any time. If the teachers were encouraged by their program to converse in this manner all day every day, they would make a very large dent in the infamous thirty-million-word gap by the end of the school year. If they showed parents how to do the same, the language gap might disappear altogether.

Unfortunately, the characterization of early childhood classrooms as places where "even teachers who work under such constraints can still decide to talk and act like human beings" may be a bit over optimistic. Under the withering attack of the accountability model, more and more teachers are not only expected to remain on schedule and follow the activities as provided by the curriculum, they are also required to stick with a predetermined script for every activity. Reading a book, for example, which should be a springboard for language, has started to become in some programs an entirely scripted activity in which teacher-child interaction is limited to the prescribed comments and the required questions that are provided by the ready-made lesson plan.

That would be the opposite of the language-rich classroom.

The Dignity of Children's Play

Adults have occupations. Children have play. Adults want to be taken seriously and respected for what they do. So do children. Play is as purposeful and important to them as any adult endeavor. Play is the place in the child's life in which he is the decision maker and the problem solver.

Building a house, taking care of babies, driving a truck, taking a patient's pulse and listening to a heartbeat, teaching school, arresting bad guys—such are among the many grown-up tasks taken on by the child in play. To the child, all of this is serious business. When adults take play seriously, they also take the child seriously and find opportunity not only to communicate meaningfully but also to afford the child the dignity so conspicuously absent in so many of his interactions with the adult world.

The early childhood profession recognizes the importance of play. On the true-false Scantron score sheet that aspiring early childhood educators (including those who went on to earn PhDs and now occupy places of great influence in the early childhood arena) had to complete on their first exam for Child Development 101, most students were able to reply accurately to the statement "Young children learn best through play."

Everybody gets the question right, but does anybody actually believe it?

On the one hand, a very visible sign that most programs value play is the money spent on stuff to play with, which is quite a lot. Most classrooms have shelves and shelves packed with blocks, trucks, art materials, games, puppets, flannel boards, dolls, dress-up clothes, and furnishings for make-believe play—such as stoves, refrigerators, sinks, and child-size couches—as well as tricycles, balls, and climbing equipment for outdoor play.

On the other hand, the most visible sign that the program does not value play is the typical daily schedule that is as jam-packed as the toys on the shelves. A great deal of time and energy are spent on the many required tasks—large groups, small groups, meals, snacks, walks down the hallway to the bathrooms—and an almost equal amount of time and energy devoted to moving children from task to task. "I need you to . . . line up, clean up, sit down, lie down, come here, put that away, stop doing that, go there, pick that up." Chief among the many mixed messages teachers receive about what constitutes quality early childhood education are the simultaneous admonishments to minimize management talk but to follow a daily schedule that demands management talk all day long.

Children who come into the classroom in wide-eyed aston-ishment at all of the amazing possibilities soon learn the bitter truth. There's a lot of stuff to play with, but it's never time to play. Well, almost never. Almost every early childhood program has a block of time during which the toy store is open. Playtime goes by different names, one of which is "choice" time. It is, in theory, a part of the daily schedule that might actually provide oppor-tunities for adults to converse and during which teachers might be encouraged to depart from scripted lessons, to use teachable moments, and to ask open-ended questions. But as one might well imagine, a great deal of pent-up energy is released when the appointed moment arrives, and because every child in the classroom is trying to use the same materials at the same time, the competition for space, materials, and attention is fierce. The adult role is quickly reduced to directing traffic, resolving con-flicts, and engaging in "drive-by" interactions.

"Only four people are allowed in this center at a time, Jamie. You don't belong here." "Christopher, use your walking feet."

"Maria, use your words. Tell him you don't like that."

"Tell me about your drawing, Tyrone. It's your family? That's nice. Christopher, please don't climb on that shelf."

"Tell me about your building, Joshua. A house? That's nice. Pedro, you need to wipe your nose and wash your hands."

Teachable moments during child-directed play are no more pro-ductive than those used by Ms. White during the teacher-directed pumpkin activity, and for the same reasons. Yes, the questions are responsive to the child's interest, but the content is still driven not by a desire to communicate but by the pressure to teach early learning performance objectives. Thanks to learning standards, when children play with blocks, for example, teachers routinely ask, "What shape is it? Is it a triangle or a rectangle?" (Answer: it's the same shape that it was yesterday!) and occasionally, "How many blocks high is the tower?" When children play make-believe and pretend to cook pepperoni pizza, the predictable question is, "What food group is this? Is it a vegetable or a fruit?"

Notice how often in this reductionist version of the teachable moment the question is phrased in binary form. Teachers don't always ask directly about a particular concept but will instead pose alternatives, such as "Is the oatmeal soft or crunchy?" "Is it raining outside, or is it sunny?" "Do flowers bloom in spring or in winter?"

Teachers are not trained to address children in this manner, but it is a way of talking to children that is deeply embedded in the culture of early childhood education. One possible source of this style of questioning is a curriculum that provides lessons in binary format so that teachers often find themselves teaching concepts such as "on and off" and "full and empty." Or perhaps the curricula are not at fault. Perhaps in college the teacher had to complete one too many Scantrons. No matter what the reason, in a typical classroom during breakfast, after the teacher dishes out another serving of scrambled eggs, the teachable moment is often reduced to "Do you have more, or do you have less?"

Waste a child's precious and irretrievable early years teaching "less" and "more," and the child will always learn less.

Interviewing Children vs.
Having Conversations with Them

By enquiring about shapes and food groups, teachers demonstrate that they are not really interested in what children are building, cooking, pretending, drawing, or fashioning out of playdough.

These activities are only valuable in that they provide opportunities to conduct the ongoing quiz.

Teachers, of course, aren't supposed to quiz children about full and empty, shapes and colors—at least during play. The preferred format is the open-ended question.

"Tell me about what you're building," a teacher asks a child during choice time in the block center.

"A house," the child replies.

The purpose of the open-ended question is to provide opportunities for the child to think about his answer, to express ideas, to respond with more than one word, to be creative, and to use a larger vocabulary. Naturally, then, the teacher had expected more of a response than "A house." Although it was not what she had hoped for, she resists the temptation to hit-and-run with a quick "That's nice," and instead she asks a follow-up question, hoping for a better result.

"A house! Who lives in the house?"

"My family."

The teacher pauses. Now what?

"Your family! What do they do?"

"Watch TV."

A longer pause, then, "Watch TV? Tell me what they watch."

"*Judge Judy.*"

The teacher surrenders. "That's nice," she says.

Here is someone who with the best of intentions had implemented what she had been taught were best practices in helping children learn to communicate, but who had walked away from this encounter feeling oddly deflated. All of her questions had more than one right answer. They were personally meaningful. What happened to all the language that open-ended questions are supposed to produce?

What the child understands about this encounter, although she cannot yet articulate it, is that it is not a normal human conversation—it is an interview, as contrived, perfunctory, awkward, and pointless as those she will be required to respond to for the rest of her childhood. "How old are you? What grade are you in? Where do you go to school? Do you like your teacher?" End of interview.

Standards-driven early childhood education is not only that it reduces complex human behavior such as communication and critical thinking to observable micro-steps, thereby rendering it useless, but that it reduces the child to nothing more than a set of objectives, a collection of deficits, a problem.

The problem with standards-driven early childhood education is not only that it reduces complex human behavior such as communication and critical thinking to observable micro-steps, thereby rendering it useless, but that it reduces the child to nothing more than a set of objectives, a collection of deficits, a problem that eternally needs fixing. The "Who lives in the house?" interview above demonstrates to the child that despite her persistence, the teacher has no more interest in who the child is than the teacher who dismisses Consuela and her mama's smile. True, it is a step up from "What color is the pumpkin?" but ultimately it is nothing more than a somewhat more artful manipulation of the child, designed to ascertain the only things we do care about—what does she know, what can she do, and where does it fit into the assessment of her progress toward "school readiness."

Her teacher likes to ask questions, but she isn't really interested in the house.

Where was the language? It is a better question to ask of the teacher, not the child. The child has only been on the planet for four years and does not have a great deal of experience in holding up her end of a conversation, much less responding to an interview. Given those circumstances, she acquitted herself quite well.

The Value of Authentic Communication

Let us imagine how different this encounter might be if the teacher had no agenda whatsoever when she approaches the child. She is someone who is simply in the habit of talking to children as if they were human beings. It might look something like this.

"Tell me about what you're building."

"A house."

"Well, make sure you include lots of bedrooms. When I was little I had to share my bedroom with my sister, and I never had any privacy."

"My mama needs her privacy in the bathroom."

"Me, too! I always wished I could live in a house where I could have my own bathroom. Do you want to put a bathroom in this house just for your mom?"

"That's silly."

"Really? What's so ridiculous about my idea?"

"Because sometimes I need to use the bathroom, too."

"Well, then, what can we do to ensure your mother's privacy?"

"We could lock the bathroom door!"

"I see. So a family bathroom is okay just as long as it's one at a time."

"Yep."

And so on.

As this interaction continues, the teacher joins the child in play and helps build the house. She might note that the short cylindrical blocks make nice round kitchen tables; she might count the bedrooms, and, as they work together, they might even decide to sell the house instead of live in it. If so, the teacher could take a picture of it and pin it on the wall or post it on the Internet with the following caption:

For Sale by Owner. Four BR.
One bath. Two million dollars.
Call 270-555-3691

What just happened? The standards-driven educator would be completely baffled by the above interaction. It was cute, perhaps, but in what ways did it move the child closer to school readiness or prepare her to compete in the global economy? What were the objectives? Where is the assessment in this process? What did the child learn?

There are lots of ways to answer those questions, but in order to help our educator friend understand what just happened, perhaps we should use an approach that makes sense to her. Let's break it down into small pieces. But rather than write objectives about what the child will learn or do—she learns way faster than our objectives might capture—let's write objectives about what the teacher will say and do.

First of all, notice that it is the adult, not the child who carries the conversation. In the brief encounter before they begin building together, the teacher uses one hundred words, the child twenty-eight. This is as it should be. What did the NAEYC say about the language gap—that children in poverty hear far fewer words? They do not say that children in poverty are *taught* far fewer words but that they *hear* far fewer words. So, if we must have objectives, then let us begin with these.

Objective 1: "The teacher will use words in meaningful contexts."

Second, note that out of ten sentences spoken by the adult, only four are questions, and each of the questions asked is a natural follow-up to where the child took the conversation. It begins with "Tell me about what you're building," an opening gambit as natural as "How are you? How's your family? Did you have a good vacation?"

The second question, "Do you want to put a bathroom in this house just for your mom?" is somewhat misleading, because taken out of context, it sounds like a yes or no question—the kind we try to avoid. In context, however, we see that the adult is modeling problem solving and brainstorming. The child's mother needs privacy in the bathroom. Because the teacher is invested in the play for its own sake and does not see it simply as a platform by which she can teach concepts, she wants to build a house that meets the needs of its occupants. A bathroom for the mom seems like a good option.

When the child shoots her idea down, she asks, "What's so ridiculous about my idea?" It is a question that demands that the child defend her position. If she is going to tell someone her idea is no good, she needs to be able to say why. It is a question that requires the child to think analytically.

The child's answer is a window into her thinking and her experience. At age four, she cannot conceive of a house that has more than one bathroom, and she is not about to hand it over to her mom.

The fourth question, "Well, then, what can we do to ensure your mother's privacy?" now asks the child to engage in problem solving in ways that are meaningful to the child, which she does quite well, arriving at a solution much more economical and efficient than building a whole new bathroom.

Objective 2: The teacher will ask questions to promote problem solving and critical thinking.

Notice that the first question, "Tell me about what you're building," draws a minimal response: "A house." If this teacher had asked another question immediately, she would be well on her way to another pointless interview. Instead, she describes her own experiences with houses and the lessons she has learned from living in them. *It is this sharing of her own story that elicits language from the child—not the next open-ended question.* Recall that when the two teachers in the break room shared their stories about their families over a cup of coffee, not a single question was asked. In communication mode, humans volunteer their stories when they hear someone else volunteer theirs.

This child may or may not come from a language-rich home, but she is at age four quite familiar with the conventions of authentic discourse and able to participate in it when provided the opportunity. What else does the NAEYC tell us that the children of poverty lack? The opportunity to participate in extended conversations.

Objective 3: The teacher will share personal stories with the child that draw the child into extended conversations.

Notice that there is nothing dumbed down in this conversation for easy consumption by the preschool child. The teacher uses the same long, complex sentences that she uses when she speaks to an adult. She uses an adult vocabulary, and she does not stop to explain words such as *privacy, ensure, ridiculous,* or *cylindrical* but has confidence that the child will figure out their meaning as they are used in context.

Objective 4: The adult will use complex sentence structure and a rich vocabulary.

Also notice the inclusion of "academic" information in the house-building fantasy. Numerals, letters, counting, printed words, shapes, and personal information are all introduced in the context of the job in front of the two builders (teacher and child) to build and sell a house. Every builder and every buyer wants to know how many bedrooms a house has. The builder needs to use printed words in order to advertise her product, and she needs to provide her phone number.

Objective 5: The teacher will provide opportunities for children to use print and numeracy in ways that are personally meaningful.

In contrast, each of the previous examples throughout this book of teacher-child interactions and the introduction of academic concepts such as letters, numbers, colors, shapes, food groups, and so on occur in ways that have no meaning or context and therefore short circuit what may have become language-rich experiences.

It's a good lesson plan only if we keep in mind that none of it was planned but remember instead that these and numerous other objectives around language, critical thinking, literacy, and math are only subject to deconstruction *after the fact*. They did not occur because the teacher had a checklist of objectives; they occurred because the teacher was interested in building a house. Not once does the teacher ask herself, "What is it that I am teaching right now?" She listens to what the child has to say, and just as if she were talking to a friend, a coworker, or a spouse, she shares her experiences and her opinions.

It is a different way of being.

Chapter 5

Amelia's Story: Recognizing That Every Child Is Different

Chapter 3 illustrates how children change rapidly during their early years and how early childhood education struggles to respond to the wide differences in children's developmental abilities across and within age groups. This chapter examines instead the ways that children do not change—those characteristics of human beings that appear in infancy and tend to remain constant over time. It is the story of how a child's preschool program is unable to respond to who she is, the futility of her program's efforts to change her into someone she is not, and the damage caused by the inability to treat children as individuals.

The idea that young children have individual qualities that are resistant to change is not a new one. J. Ronald Lally (1990, 2013) has advocated tirelessly for decades that programs serving infants and toddlers be more responsive to individual temperaments. This chapter will do the same but will focus on preschool and will use the word *temperament* in a broader sense than those formal categories identified by Dr. Lally.

A motivational speaker was invited to address the employees of a software development firm whose main task was to write code day in and day out. He was initially quite offended when he saw that most of his audience had not only brought their laptops with them but never once looked up from their screens during his entire address. Afterward he discovered they were all looking at the same web page the entire time—the live streaming of his speech over the Internet.

They weren't trying to be rude. They were interested in his speech. They just found it uncomfortable to look him in the eye.

Some might refer scornfully to that audience as geeks or nerds, but it would be more accurate and respectful to simply say they are people who are not comfortable with a great deal of social contact. If we got to know them, we would discover that many of them had been this way from their childhoods for as far back as they could remember. If you asked their parents, they would tell you how completely different they were from their siblings, even during infancy. The sibling would smile at every adult he met. His mother could hand him to a stranger in an elevator while she straightened her stocking and he would coo and goo.

But the future code writer? His mother couldn't hand him to her own mother, even though her mother lived with her. He would scream and arch his back and not be placated until he was back in his mother's arms.

Everybody's different. The person who thrives on social inter-action and the person who tries to avoid it are two examples, but there are others. Some people hate to be told what to do and experience high levels of stress in settings in which they have little autonomy and are micromanaged. Others, however, find security in authority and rules and feel most comfortable when they know exactly what behavior is required and are able to comply with those requirements.

Some people crave predictability. They need agendas and itineraries. When they go out of town for a vacation, they go online to find out everything a certain locale has to offer and will not feel satisfied with their trip unless they visit every spot. Other folks much prefer the unexpected and find the greatest satisfaction in wandering aimlessly and letting life come to them. Some folks love Disney World for all of its many choices of things to do and for the busy hum of activity. Other folks hate it for the very same reasons. They are overwhelmed by all the things they might do and all of the coming and going. Given a choice, they would rather be under an umbrella at the beach with a good book.

Temperaments, preferences, and interests show up quite early in life, but it takes time for children to figure out who they are and what they like. It also takes time for children to develop strategies for accommodating their individual needs and to find settings in which they feel most at home. The noncompliant child grows up and hopefully finds a work environment where she has a great deal of autonomy and lots of choices. The loner finds a job that minimizes the need to interact. Not everyone finds settings where they feel at home, but as they mature they learn to live with the stress and discomfort of being out of place.

Temperaments, preferences, and interests show up quite early in life, but it takes time for children to figure out who they are and what they like.

The Story of Four-Year-Old Amelia: A Cautionary Tale

Young children often do not feel at home in institutional settings, but they lack the maturity to articulate their needs, and they have no strategies for coping with who they are and where they find themselves. Four-year-old Amelia is a classic example:

- She is noncompliant.
- She likes to play alone or with only one or two children.
- She does not bond easily with adults other than her parents.
- She likes a slow pace and needs time for long, uninterrupted play.
- She is a daydreamer.
- She is cautious.
- She loves books and loves to play with dolls.
- She has a low tolerance for frustration.

One Saturday afternoon her daddy is home alone with her while her mother runs errands. Daddy turns on the baseball game, but after the first inning, he notices that Amelia has been very quiet. It's always a bit alarming when a four-year-old child has been quiet for a while, so Daddy goes back to her room to see what mischief she is up to.

Her door is ajar, and her back is turned so she doesn't see Daddy looking over her shoulder. She has Ken in one hand, Barbie in the other. Although Amelia is not making a sound, Daddy can see that Barbie and Ken are deep in conversation by the way Amelia shakes one doll and then the other. The happy couple decide to go to the beach, and when the two of them hop into the Barbie Glam Convertible with a surfboard and a beach ball, Daddy realizes there is a story unfolding and that there is a setting of sand and water and palm trees invisible to him.

The second inning has begun. Relieved that Amelia is not wandering in the street or playing in the toilet, Daddy sneaks back to his baseball game. Amelia remains in her room until the seventh inning, when she comes into the living room and announces she is hungry.

"There's yogurt in the refrigerator," Daddy reminds her.

Daddy believes in self-help.

Amelia is a picky eater, not one to try new foods, so from the time her parents discovered she would eat yogurt, they have kept the refrigerator well stocked.

Amelia has her snack and climbs up on Daddy's lap with her favorite book, *Jennie's Hat*.

"Daddy, will you read to me?"

"Sure thing." Daddy mutes the ball game. "What have you got there? Ezra Jack Keats?"

Amelia nods her head.

Daddy reads the book. When Jennie's aunt is introduced, Amelia interrupts the story to talk about her own aunt Karen. Daddy tells the story of spending the night at his aunt Carmelita's house by the railroad track when he was little and how lonesome the train whistle sounded. Amelia tells him that when Barbie is lonesome, she always calls up Ken.

Before they get to the end of the book, Amelia grows tired of it and tells Daddy she wants to watch cartoons. Daddy says she can watch cartoons after the baseball game is over.

"That's not fair!" Amelia wails, and throws herself on the floor. Daddy has to turn his head so she doesn't see him laugh. When Daddy turns up the volume on the ball game and acts completely oblivious to her fit, Amelia eventually concedes defeat and stomps back to her room. Later, when Daddy calls her to tell her the ball game is over, she is in the middle of drawing a picture of a train and says, "That's okay. I don't want to watch TV."

It is an ordinary afternoon on any Saturday. Amelia is at home, where she is completely accepted for who she is, and no one would ever think there was anything about her that needs fixing or that anything should happen any differently. When Daddy sees that she is deep in play, he doesn't interrupt her concentration to ask her about what color Ken's shirt is. He doesn't flip her light switch on and off and tell her Barbie time is over and it's time to put her dolls away so they can have story time. He doesn't worry that she likes to play by herself, and he doesn't try to round up a couple more four-year-old children from the neighborhood so that Amelia can learn social skills. When she's hungry, he doesn't tell her it's not time for snack. He reads the book when asked, but he is in no hurry to finish, nor does he insist that she stay in his lap when she grows tired of the book. He responds to her tantrum with patience and humor. It does not occur to him that she might need the services of a child psychologist.

Everything changes on Monday morning.

Amelia's Struggles in Preschool

Amelia's preschool classroom is considered to be a good one. The teacher has a four-year degree in early childhood education. She likes children, and she likes her job. The curriculum and the assessment instrument provided to this classroom are widely used and well respected in the world of early childhood and have been specifically designed to support the statewide school readiness goals for four-year-old children. The daily schedule was developed by the school district's early childhood specialist and is used throughout the school system. There are lots of materials and activities to explore. This particular classroom is seen as a model of success because the data demonstrates that the average student in this classroom moves on to kindergarten having successfully accomplished over 90 percent of the expected school readiness performance objectives.

Monday morning is the beginning of Amelia's fifth week of school. During that first month, Amelia's teacher, Ms. Kruczynski, has formally identified a wide range of performance objectives Amelia needs to work on. She has also become acutely aware that Amelia is noncompliant, prefers to be alone, does not bond easily with her teachers, hates to be interrupted, loves dolls, has a short fuse, and doesn't like to try new things. Almost all of Amelia's characteristics are the exact opposite of the template of temperament, learning styles, interests, and abilities that mark the "successful" child, and Ms. Kruczynski has made it her job to give Amelia the necessary makeover that will help her fit in and achieve success.

Ms. Kruczynski has made it her job to give Amelia the necessary makeover that will help her fit in and achieve success.

For starters, Amelia obviously hates being here and would much prefer to stay at home. She cries when she boards the bus in the morning and has to be physically strapped into her seat. Although the majority of the other children have already formed attachments to Ms. Kruczynski and will hug her as soon as they arrive, Amelia is slow to bond with strange adults. She arrives in the classroom resentful and suspicious, not at all happy to see her teacher.

Truth be told, Ms. Kruczynski is not all that thrilled to see Amelia either. Ms. Kruczynski thrives on the kind of unconditional love only small children and puppies seem to have in their emotional repertoire. She has already notified her supervisor that Amelia is suffering from *separation anxiety*, a clinical term that in early-childhood-speak means "loves her mother" or "strongly prefers the unqualified acceptance of parents and the security of home to institutional life."

Amelia's noncompliant streak also makes her ill suited to classroom life. Ms. Kruczynski has reported to her supervisor that Amelia is defiant and has asked for some behavior modification strategies for dealing with the defiant child. Ms. Kruczynski is mistaken, however, to equate defiance with noncompliance. Defiant is not who Amelia *is*. It is a description of what she *does* because she has not yet learned any other strategies. It is only one of many possible options available to the individual who hates being told what to do. The four-year-old child simply has fewer of those options at her disposal than does the adult. Ms. Kruczynski of all people should realize this because she is noncompliant herself. When given a direct command, Ms. Kruczynski will not always directly disobey but will choose her response based on her *evaluation of the consequences* of defiance. If the school principal tells her she is on bus monitor duty, she reports for bus monitor duty, even though she despises it. If the state trooper on the interstate directs traffic to the off-ramp because of road conditions, Ms. Kruczynski turns onto the off-ramp, even though she is in a hurry and is quite certain she is perfectly capable of dealing with the road conditions. But if her grouchy next-door neighbor yells at her from his driveway to rake her leaves because he doesn't like living next door to the Addams Family, she will respond with a rude gesture. No one is going to tell Ms. Kruczynski when to rake her leaves.

Amelia, at age four, does not have the capacity to weigh the consequences of disobedience. If her decision to resist or to comply with a direct command has any criteria at all, it is how badly she wants to do something she has been told not to do. More often

> *D*efiant is not who Amelia is. *It is a description of what she* does *because she has not yet learned any other strategies.*

than not, though, her disobedience is a function of her mood and how tired she is. On some days her mother can walk into Amelia's room and say, "Amelia, pick your clothes up off the floor," and Amelia will cheerfully comply.

But if Amelia is overtired, her mother can make the same request in the same tone of voice, and Amelia will cry, "Stop yelling at me!" If she is deep in play and her mother interrupts her to do a simple housekeeping chore, she is apt to wail, "That's not fair!" and then go into a deep pout. Four-year-old Amelia is not choosing these responses; they are choosing her.

But adult Ms. Kruczynski is quite capable of choosing the way she responds to authority, and one of the specific outcomes she will consider is the likelihood of getting caught should she choose to break a rule. It was the guiding criteria most prominent during her adolescence when she used to sneak cigarettes in the bathroom or meet her boyfriend at the fast-food joint when she was supposed to be studying with a friend. This strategy is still very much in play in Ms. Kruczynski's adult life as well. In her current job, for example, there is an ironclad rule forbidding the use of cell phones in the classroom. Ms. Kruczynski keeps her cell phone in her pocket on silent mode and furtively checks her text messages every so often to see how many messages her sister has sent. Her sister keeps Ms. Kruczynski's two-year-old daughter, Melissa. Try as she might, Ms. Kruczynski has been unable to help her sister distinguish the relative importance of "She just used the potty again!" from "Meet me at the ER!" so Ms. Kruczynski has to plow through a lot of messages just in case.

Amelia applies the same logic to disobedience as well, but from a four-year-old's perspective, that never quite works out for her. If she sneaks the last piece of her sister's birthday cake while her sister is on an overnight visit, it doesn't occur to her that the circumstantial evidence against her would be fairly compelling. When she tries to circumvent authority in the classroom when she thinks no one is looking, she invariably gets caught. In a preschool classroom, someone is always looking.

A catalog of Ms. Kruczynski's noncompliant adult responses would not be complete without a nod to her passive-aggressive behavior, which she has down to a science. When her supervisor, Ms. Lute, announces the no-cell-phone policy at a staff meeting, Ms. Kruczynski does not raise her hand and ask if there could be exceptions for important text messages from home that could be checked at a specified time so as not to distract the classroom staff from the job at hand. Instead, she nods her head in agreement, even though she has no intention of obeying that particular policy. When Ms. Lute conducts her annual classroom observation, she suggests that Ms. Kruczynski not line the children up at the sink to wash their hands before breakfast but instead send them to the sink one at a time in order to minimize the disruptive behavior the boys at the end of the line display when they have nothing to do but wait. And perhaps the girls should not always get to wash their hands first. Ms. Kruczynski does not say, "Children need to learn how to wait their turn whether they have anything to do or not, and if I let the boys go first, they'll play with their dishes and silverware at the table while they wait for the girls to finish washing their hands." Instead, she thanks Ms. Lute for her suggestions and tells her how much she welcomes constructive criticism.

Amelia, in her own four-year-old way, will likewise often agree to comply with a specific instruction only to disregard it later, but she is not nearly so calculating. She is sincere when she agrees not to give the cloth baby doll a bath in the water center, but when the opportunity presents itself, she just cannot help herself.

Of all the strategies Ms. Kruczynski has at her disposal, her choice of career has served her the best. True, employment in a school system comes with a zillion rules, but her supervisor only observes her once a year, and as long as she keeps her paperwork up to date, she exercises a great deal of autonomy in how she runs her classroom on a daily basis.

And the four-year-old equivalent of that strategy? Well, there is no four-year-old equivalent of that strategy.

Trying to Make Amelia into Someone She Is Not

The classroom is a haven of sorts for Ms. Kruczynski, but it is a disaster for Amelia. Perhaps someday when she is grown, Amelia will find a job that allows her to work in her pajamas in front of a laptop where, as in the Beatles' "Octopus's Garden," there will be no one there to tell her what to do. But not today. At age four, when she is least equipped to understand her own temperament or to deal with it appropriately, she finds herself in an environment in which she will be more micromanaged than at any other time in her life. Even though she complies more often than not, it is not often enough to satisfy the demands of institutional life. The teacher, pressured by the misguided demands of school readiness, is unable to offer Amelia any strategies that might ease her path, and by default, Amelia, the noncompliant child, becomes Amelia, the defiant child.

It begins the minute she walks in the door.

Amelia rides the blue bus, and by the time she arrives, the children on the green and red buses have already gathered on the carpet with Ms. Kruczynski's assistant, Ms. Bates, to mull over today's weather and calendar (important items on the kindergarten checklist). Ms. Kruczynski greets children as they arrive, reminding them to hang up their coats and to join the other children on the carpet.

It is a scene repeated in preschool and Head Start classrooms all over the United States. Some classrooms gather the children first thing in the morning for story time, some for songs and movement, some for weather and calendar, but regardless of the specific activity, the name of the game remains the same. It is called "Keep Them Busy until Breakfast."

Amelia doesn't want to join the group—groups make her feel stressed and uncomfortable. (It's tough to be a loner in a setting in which even going to the bathroom is a social activity.) But Ms. Kruczynski is a professional. She knows Amelia is not happy, so this morning she tries something different.

"Amelia, I know you're not happy here, but I want to remind you about how much fun we're going to have today. Let's take a little tour of the classroom so you can think about what you might want to do."

Amelia accepts the proffered hand and allows her teacher to show her around. "Here's the art center," Ms. Kruczynski says. "I've seen you coloring before. Maybe today you'd like to try to paint. And here's dramatic play. I know you love the baby dolls."

Amelia mistakes this observation as an invitation. She cannot believe her good fortune. Everyone else is on the carpet trying to decide if today is Monday or Christmas, and she will have the dolls all to herself. She releases her teacher's hand and makes a beeline for the learning center.

"Oh, Amelia, I'm sorry. It's not time for learning centers yet. Look at the schedule." Ms. Kruczynski points to the illustrated schedule posted on the wall. "You can choose this center at ten o'clock, right after we're finished with our small group." Ten o'clock is over two hours away, which in four-year-old time is roughly the equivalent of about two and a half Ice Ages.

"Come on, Amelia, I need you to come to the carpet with the rest of the children."

Doing the same thing at the same time with the rest of the children rates very high on the list of school readiness goals in this classroom. It is the source of many a confrontation, including this one.

Amelia manages to overcome her disappointment but still tries out the "maybe no one is looking" strategy when she brings one of the dolls with her to the carpet. No dice. This time it is Ms. Bates who issues the instruction.

"Give me the doll please, Amelia. You know the rules. Our dolls belong in the dramatic play center." When Amelia is not forthcoming, Ms. Bates wrests it from her grasp.

"That's not fair!" Amelia cries, throwing herself on the carpet.

Ms. Bates and Ms. Kruczynski exchange weary looks. Ms. Kruczynski makes a note to report these outbursts to the school psychologist.

A cart on wheels carrying the morning meal rolls into the classroom at eight o'clock. Ms. Kruczynski instructs the children to line up at the sink, girls first, to wash their hands, which takes a long time. Amelia is at the front of the line; she washes her hands and sits at the breakfast table waiting for the others to finish. To entertain herself, she wears her bowl on her head like a bonnet, which draws a swift reprimand, as does the pushing and shoving of the boys waiting at the back of the line with nothing to do.

The children are having oatmeal this morning. Amelia is not hungry, and although she has never tried oatmeal, she is quite sure she doesn't like it. Ms. Kruczynski has anticipated this response from Amelia and is ready for her.

"Oh, I like the way Victor is eating his oatmeal. And I like the way Tanya is eating her oatmeal, and I like the way . . ." This goes around the table until the way every child is eating oatmeal is liked, except for Amelia, of course, who is not eating her oatmeal. "Come on, Amelia, won't you give it a try?"

Amelia gives it a try. She takes a spoonful. Even if she did like it, she would never admit it, but she feels that she has been cooperative beyond the call of duty. Having earned the "I like the way . . ." salutation fair and square, Amelia gets up from the table and heads for the baby dolls. The daily schedule, however, does not say, "Children may be excused from the table when they have finished eating." It says that breakfast for every child lasts thirty minutes. Ms. Kruczynski and Ms. Bates, fearful that Amelia's departure will set off a stampede to the learning centers, insist that Amelia return to her seat. Again the noncompliant child obeys the direct command, albeit with her bottom lip sticking out and her arms crossed.

Breakfast is supposed to be prime time for unscripted interaction, and Ms. Kruczynski does her best to stimulate conversation. She runs through the gamut of binary food questions—hot or cold, sweet or sour, sweet or salty, followed by food groups and colors. Those topics exhausted, Ms. Kruczynski asks what we use to smell our food, taste our food, and see our food, and reminds the children that these are three of our five senses. If Amelia knew how to roll her eyes, she would. Why do her teachers talk this way, and why do they make her listen?

Breakfast mercifully ends, and as children depart from the breakfast table, Amelia's quite predictable foray into the dramatic play center is short-circuited. It's time once again for the children to gather on the carpet. This time Amelia is so frustrated she refuses to leave. Her teacher, equally frustrated, carries her to the carpet, where she is told not only to sit, but where to sit (on your spot), how to sit (legs crossed, hands in lap), and how long to sit (until story time is over). Talk about micromanagement!

"Children, our book this morning is *Jennie's Hat*." Amelia's ears perk up, but the book reading quickly descends into tedium. "The name of the book is also called what?" (Some think the name of the book is called *Jennie's Hat*, but they are mistaken.) "The name of the book is called the *title*." And what do we call the person who wrote the book? "The *au* . . . the *au* . . . the *au-thor*. That's right children, the person who writes a book is called the *au-thor*." And so it goes, through *ill* . . . *ill* . . . *ill* . . . *ill-us-tra-tor*, title page, front of the book, back of the book, and spine—performance objectives every one.

Amelia has listened to this same recitation every morning for a month. She is quite sure she can't stand to hear another word of it. (Little does she realize that the limits of her endurance will be tested beyond all imagination as this same ritual is repeated every morning for the rest of the year. Amelia is just lucky she didn't start preschool when she was three.) The child sitting next to Amelia gets into her space. Amelia irritably pushes him back onto his spot.

"Amelia, you might not like this book, but I'm sure your friend does. Please leave him alone so he can enjoy the book."

Amelia is not the only child completely uninvolved with this kind of reading of the story, and her teacher has to stop repeatedly to reprimand and redirect children, which makes the reading of the book last twice as long as is indicated on the daily schedule. Everyone, including the teacher, heaves a sigh of relief when it finally ends. What's next on the schedule? Small group. Amelia is very interested in small group, whatever that might be, because she remembers her teacher's promise.

"You can choose this center at ten o'clock, right after we're finished with our small group."

Today's small group is handprints, an activity in which children place their hands in a shallow tray of tempera paint and make a handprint on a roll of butcher paper that will be displayed in the hallway right outside the classroom. Amelia and Jacob, the boy sitting next to her, think exactly the same thing: "I can't believe I'm going to put my hand in paint." Their meanings, however, are completely opposite. Jacob thinks this is the coolest thing he has ever seen. He hopes he gets to make a thousand handprints. Amelia is not only very cautious by nature and thus very unlikely to put her hands into anything the least bit out of the ordinary, but her mother is an artist, and Amelia is quite sure that a paintbrush is the necessary instrument for applying paint to paper. Amelia puts her hands behind her back.

Jacob is supremely disappointed. He gets a chance to make only one print before he has to give Amelia her turn. Ms. Kruczynski is well aware of Amelia's aversion to trying new things, and she is ready for her. Ms. Kruczynski plays the mama card.

"Amelia, Jacob's mother is going to visit our classroom, and she is going to be so proud to see Jacob's handprint on the classroom wall. And Juanita's mother is going to visit the classroom, and she is going to be so proud to see Juanita's handprint on the wall. But when Amelia's mother visits the classroom, she is going to be so sad. She won't be able to find Amelia's handprint anywhere."

Amelia considers this. She knows her mom. And she knows that her teacher is not quite right. Her mother won't be sad. She'll be mad. "Why didn't *my* daughter get a chance to make a handprint?" she will demand.

Amelia decides to take one for the home team. She plops her hand into the tray of paint. (It feels just as nasty as she had feared.) She presses it quickly onto the butcher paper and holds it up in the air so her teacher can wipe the paint off as quickly as possible.

She refuses to answer any questions about how many fingers (the same as Jacob's) or what color (the same as Jacob's), and instead, her obligation to her mother satisfied, Amelia heads straight for the dramatic play center.

"And this time no one can stop me," she thinks. "It says so right on the daily schedule!"

Wrong.

It's back to the carpet again, where the children have gathered to await further instructions. For this segment of the day, children are expected to sit quietly on their spots until called on by their teacher, at which time they announce in which learning center they wish to play. Amelia, who has been announcing her choice all morning long must participate in this ritual before she can actually play with the dolls. Those who "sit nicely" are allowed to choose first. Amelia is not sitting nicely, and all the children have already left the carpet for their respective destinations by the time it is her turn to choose.

It has been a long morning for teacher and child. Amelia, the child who likes to play alone, has spent the day in the company of nineteen other children with not a moment of respite. The child who hates to be told what to do has been ordered around like a buck private at boot camp; the child who hates interruptions has complied with a schedule that is nothing but a series of interruptions. The child who needs to fantasize and daydream has not been afforded that opportunity for even a minute.

And the dramatic play center? It is not just the place where Amelia can pursue her interest in dolls. It is a place where she can escape the crowd, where she can exercise control over her own world, where she can disappear into a world of her own making. It is the one place in the classroom where she can be herself. From the moment she walked through the door this morning, her inability to find safe haven in dramatic play has raised her stress level continuously with every passing moment.

But she is not the only one experiencing stress. Ms. Kruczynski has spent the morning pursuing the thankless and impossible task of trying to make Amelia into someone she is not—someone who could be molded to fit the template of the child who is successful in institutional life. As Ms. Kruczynski appraises her problem child who is waiting in a deep pout on the carpet, a scowl etched across her countenance, Ms. Kruczynski is not sure who needs medication most, her or Amelia.

But Ms. Kruczynski is a professional, and she gathers herself one more time.

"Amelia, where would you like to play?" she asks evenly, as if it were a secret.

Amelia does not look up or change her expression. She points to the dolls.

"Do you mean the dramatic play center?"

Amelia nods. She does.

"I'm sorry, Amelia. Only four children are allowed in there at a time. That center is full."

When Amelia does not reply, Ms. Kruczynski leads her to the art center. "Hang your name tag right here," she instructs Amelia, pointing to one of four plastic hooks affixed to the art center shelf. Amelia knows the system. Plastic hooks corresponding to the number of children permitted to play there are displayed prominently at every learning center. Children visiting the center hang their name tags on the hooks to announce their presence. If there is a name tag on every hook, the center is declared full and no one else may play there until a child leaves, taking his name tag with him. There are four hooks in dramatic play and four in art. All the hooks in dramatic play are occupied, but one is still available in art, which is where Ms. Kruczynski directs Amelia to hang her name tag.

Amelia sits at the art table with some watercolors but does not paint. Instead, she watches Ms. Kruczynski intently as she visits the other learning centers around the classroom. On the other side of the room, Ms. Kruczynski turns her back on the classroom for a moment to check her text messages on her smartphone. A moment is all Amelia needs. In an instant she is at the dramatic play center. Quick as lightning she removes Juanita's name tag from its hook, depositing it quickly into the trash can and replacing it on the hook with her own.

Ms. Bates is on her in a heartbeat.

"You do not belong in this center, young lady, and it is *not* nice to throw Juanita's name tag into the trash. Come with me now. You will not play in the dramatic play center for the rest of the day."

As she leads Amelia across the room, they pass an elaborate tower that Jacob has almost finished in the block center. Amelia gives it a swift kick. (Apparently she has a low tolerance for frustration.) In the blink of an eye, Amelia has earned the triple crown of defiant, aggressive, and disruptive. Unlike Twanna from chapter 3, Amelia will not be rescued by her parents. They both have service industry jobs and need the child care provided by the school's early childhood classroom. It will come at a price though. They will have to endure endless conferences and sign a steady stream of notes documenting their daughter's poor behavior. They will be pressured to have Amelia medicated for attention-deficit/hyperactivity disorder, a popular diagnosis of children who are not cut out for institutional life.

"I'm no expert," her daddy tells the platoon of professionals assembled to discuss his child with him, including teachers, psychologists, and the school principal, "but she plays with her dolls for hours; she'll work on an intricate painting until it's completed; she'll wear me out reading books. Amelia may be a lot of things, but hyperactive is not one of them. I can't agree to put her on medication." The assembled educators are not pleased. Parents are expected to go along with the program and usually do, convinced by those better educated and in positions of authority that medication is a necessary ingredient to school success.

Here's the thing.

Amelia's teacher is not a bad person. She is not a bad teacher. It is not a bad classroom. In fact, it is a quite typical classroom. Both Ms. Kruczynski and Ms. Bates run their classroom in the manner in which they have been trained to run a classroom. The one gaping hole in their practice is that they have failed to individualize. They expect children to conform to the demands of the institution, and it would not occur to them to modify the institution to conform to the needs of the child. They worry that when these children start school, the kindergarten teacher is not going to conform to the child, so they better start throwing the fastball to the face early and often.

Policy makers would be quick to point out that school readiness standards in almost every state and in the federal Head Start program explicitly require early childhood classrooms to be responsive to individual differences. They would claim that the fault here lies not with preschool but with these particular teachers, who are badly in need of additional training and perhaps closer supervision.

But Ms. Kruczynski and Ms. Bates are not alone in that point of view. The problem is that Ms. Bates, Ms. Kruczynski, and most of their colleagues believe that they *do* individualize. Gather a hundred teachers together anywhere in the country and ask them two questions: "How do you identify individual differences?" and "How do you respond to those differences?" Ninety of them will respond in terms of school readiness performance objectives. They complete the formal assessment, enter the information into the electronic database, and click the mouse—*voilà*—an individual profile for each child, each one as distinct as a finger-print. This one can count to three, that one to ten, the other to twenty. This one can cut with scissors, that one can cut on a line, and the other one doesn't know how to hold a pair of scissors. This one can follow simple instructions, that one can follow three-step commands, that one never follows any instructions.

> *To most early childhood teachers, individualization means working on different performance objectives with different children.*

Almost no one will talk about the child in terms of the child's interests, needs, learning style, or temperament.

And how do those teachers say they respond to those individual differences? Without mentioning him by name, almost every teacher will describe Tyler reductionism to a T. To most early childhood teachers, individualization means working on different performance objectives with different children.

So sure, if these teachers believe that individual differences are best identified by what the child can do and what the child knows, and not by who the child *is*, then yes, they need a lot of training. But the question in front of the early childhood profession is this: Why are so many teachers in need of the same training? And why are they so unresponsive to that training?

Chapter 6

Envisioning a Preschool Class-
room That Works for All Children

What would a classroom responsive to individual needs look like? Could it meet Amelia's needs to the point where she would no longer be considered a behavior problem? Could such a classroom successfully prepare all children for school?

Ms. Kruczynski's supervisor, Ms. Lute, believes that individualization is the key to school readiness, but has found the bureaucracy and inflexibility of the agency she works for to be suffocating. She sees in Ms. Kruczynski's frustration with Amelia an opportunity to break from the conventions and assumptions of early childhood education, but she needs to win Ms. Kruczynski over.

At Ms. Kruczynski's request, Ms. Lute observes Amelia in the classroom for a day. Afterward, she sits down with Ms. Kruczynski to make some suggestions. Let's listen to what she has to say.

Creating a New Paradigm:
Ms. Kruczynski Gets Mixed Messages

"Amelia is indeed a noncompliant person," Ms. Lute begins, "and she finds herself in such a controlled environment that defiance is often the only option available to her."

As usual, Ms. Kruczynski nods in agreement, although she is not sure where this is going.

"Ms. Kruczynski, tell me if I'm wrong, but you don't like very much to be told what to do, either, do you? And you don't seem particularly fond of rules."

Ms. Kruczynski is indignant. "Not at all. I appreciate feedback and direction."

"Really? Then why do you keep your cell phone on in the classroom?"

Jaw drops.

"And you persist in lining children up at the sink when I'm not in your classroom observing," continues Ms. Lute. "Am I right?"

Speechless.

"Girls first?"

Ms. Kruczynski nods her head weakly.

"Don't worry. You're not in trouble. When you're the supervisor, you learn to pick your battles, and this isn't one of them. What I've noticed about you, Ms. Kruczynski, is that you perform better and you are happier when I leave you alone."

Another nod, slightly less tentative.

"Amelia is just like you. She needs an environment that provides her with a great deal of autonomy. She needs to be able to make her own decisions."

"Amelia is just like you. She needs an environment that provides her with a great deal of autonomy. She needs to be able to make her own decisions."

"So what you're saying is, if she wants to be in the dramatic play center instead of morning meeting, then I should let her?" Ms. Kruczynski is incredulous.

"Yes, that would be one example."

"Does she have to eat?"

"Well none of the children have to eat. They do have to be offered food. I think you can manage to get her to the table and put some food in front of her."

"What if she takes a bite and jumps up from the table?"

"That's why we have learning centers. Encourage her to stay at the table, but don't insist. Try to engage her in conversation. Ask her about her sister. Tell her about *your* sister."

"Seriously?"

"Seriously."

"And do the same with all the groups all day long?"

"Yes."

"Okay. If that's what you want, we won't make her do anything at all. Does she have to go outside?"

"Well, you could leave her inside by herself, but then, of course, we'd all lose our jobs. And by the way, it doesn't matter what I want. When you go back to your classroom, the only thing that will matter is what you want."

Perhaps because she is so challenged by these ideas, or perhaps because she feels she has nothing to lose, Ms. Kruczynski strays from her typical passive-aggressive way of responding and speaks her mind.

"With all due respect, ma'am, I don't think you know *what* you want."

"How's that?

"Well, I don't mean you personally. I mean the school district, or the state—I don't know—the feds maybe."

"Go on."

"Well, you make us track all of these objectives all the time."

"Yes."

"Take Amelia. She's supposed to be working on staying on

task, but you're saying she doesn't have to stay on task. We want her to cooperate in group, but you say she doesn't even have to participate. We need to teach her the alphabet, but if I do an alphabet activity, Miss Amelia can just walk away from it. I know you check my lesson plans every month, and you check the progress of every child. You look to see if I have the objectives on the lesson plans and if the children have learned the lessons. So why bother to put Amelia in a lesson plan if she doesn't have to do the lesson? And how could I possibly know about her progress when she's playing with dolls all day long? She's supposed to be learning to follow a routine—it's right there on the assessment—but now you tell me she doesn't have to follow a routine. So I guess what I'm saying is this: What do you really want? Am I supposed to get her ready for school or just let her sort of hang out all day long and do whatever?"

Ms. Kruczynski stops to take a deep breath.

"So, what I hear is that you're getting mixed messages," Ms. Lute ventures.

"Big-time."

"Well, of those two choices that you just laid out, which would make *you* happiest?"

"I'm sorry?"

"How would you rather spend your time? Tracking performance objectives or playing with children?"

Ms. Kruczynski does not reply immediately. It sounds like a trick question to her. She's right. By asking her what she wants to do instead of telling her what to do, Ms. Lute is making Ms. Kruczynski take responsibility for her own practice.

Ms. Kruczynski Decides to Play with Children All Day Long

"Well, if I didn't have to worry about them being ready for school, then I'd much rather play with them."

"Okay then, play with them. I'll worry about them being ready for school."

Ms. Kruczynski's eyes narrow. "What's the catch?"

"No flies on you, Ms. Kruczynski. Yes, my offer comes with conditions. First of all, if you're going to play with them all day, then the learning centers will have to be available to them all day as well, from the moment they walk in the door until they go home."

"Okay," Ms. Kruczynski replies dubiously.

"Second, I want you to continue to plan and provide teacher-led activities that will also be available all day as well."

"How does that work?"

"Much the same as it does now. For example, I noticed on last week's plan that you did calendar and weather, you made handprints, you read a story, and during learning center time you worked with children printing their names in the writing center."

"Yes, we did other things, too. We sang songs, we did rhyming and finger play, dancing and creative movement . . ."

"So you're doing things all the time that appeal to different learning styles. That's exactly what the children need. All I'm asking you to do is to provide those activities while the learning centers are open so that children always have a choice to participate in the group or to play independently."

"Hmm." Ms. Kruczynski is thoughtful. "I'm having trouble imagining how that would work."

Ms. Lute is not surprised. "Okay. Take handprints for example. When you do the handprint activity, there's no reason to go from breakfast to the carpet, then from the carpet to the handprints, then from the small group back to the carpet, and then from the carpet back to the learning centers, and then back to the carpet again. It makes me tired just to say it. You spend all your time moving children around, and that's when you get a great deal of defiant behavior."

"That's true," Ms. Kruczynski agrees. "Amelia hates all the starting and stopping."

"So let's take Amelia," Ms. Lute suggests. "She's finishes breakfast; she gets up, clears her spot at the table, scrapes her plate, and goes to a learning center."

"Dramatic play."

"Right. So, we let the rest of the children also go directly to the centers one at a time as they finish eating."

"That will never happen," Ms. Kruczynski interjects with a trace of impatient weariness in her tone. "You don't know these kids. As soon as Amelia goes, they'll all go. In fact, if I let Amelia play in learning centers during any of my group times, they'll all want to play in learning centers. I might as well not even try to do group time."

Ms. Lute has anticipated that objection. "I know that's what you worry about—that if you don't make every child participate in the group, then no one will participate. But that assumes that every child is just the same and will act the same, which you know is not true. Every child is different. Some children love the handprint experience and would stay for a very long time if you let them; some will be interested for a while; and a few like Amelia will have to be coaxed. That's to be expected. So tomorrow, or later on that morning, you'll provide a new experience that different children, possibly even Amelia, will find compelling."

"I suppose so." Ms. Kruczynski does not sound convinced.

"And don't forget that both you and Ms. Bates have your own fan clubs—kids who just want to spend time with you whether it's at the breakfast table or making handprints or singing songs. You also have quite a few children who are naturally compliant—who will do whatever you ask because they like following the rules. So no, they won't all leave your groups or jump up from breakfast just because of what Amelia does. They all have very different temperaments and interests and will respond differently every day."

"True. But don't also forget that there are always some hardheaded children like Amelia who just want to do whatever they please." Ms. Kruczynski knows her supervisor cannot argue with that one. To her surprise, her supervisor doesn't try.

"Exactly. And by providing choices throughout the day, you will have a classroom in which every single child will feel at home."

Ms. Kruczynski isn't going to be persuaded that easily. "But don't children need to follow a schedule? Don't they need routine and predictability? Don't they need limits?"

"Of course. A child finishes breakfast. He spends a little time in conversation, but now he's ready to leave. What's the first thing he does?"

"Asks to be excused."

"Keep going."

"He scrapes his plate, throws away his trash, and then goes to . . . wherever, I guess."

"When he asks to be excused, can't you ask him where he intends to play? Couldn't you also remind him of the group activity that will be available shortly?"

"Like the handprints, for example?"

"Yes, like the handprints. Wouldn't your classroom be a more relaxed and happier place if children made their choices individually and naturally while they were leaving the breakfast table instead of waiting around on the carpet for the next thing on the schedule to begin?"

This is actually an idea that appeals to Ms. Kruczynski. Gathering eighteen children on the rug a half dozen times a day is exhausting and time consuming. Still, she is careful not to tip her hand. "Yes," she says, keeping her tone neutral, "that could work."

Ms. Lute knows that she is making progress. She plows on. "So there is your routine. Every single child eats, asks to be excused, chooses a learning center, scrapes his plate, throws his trash away, and then goes to the center. You remind each child that in a few minutes you will be doing handprints in the art center or whatever you have planned that morning, and that you'll call them when it's ready. It can't be much more predictable than that. A routine is something we do the same way every day, such as washing your hands after you go to the bathroom. It's not necessarily something that every child does at the same time."

"Okay. I see what the children are doing. But what about me and Ms. Bates? What are we doing? What's our routine?"

"Well, you multitask, conversing with children at your table while keeping an eye on the children in the centers—the same thing you do when you stop by the block center to build a house with a child. You stay engaged with that child, but you never stop scanning the classroom to make sure everyone is safe and playing productively. At breakfast, when about half of the children have gone to centers, one of you leaves the breakfast table to begin the first group activity while the other one supervises breakfast and cleanup."

"If I start handprints right after breakfast, how long do I keep it up? When do the children still at breakfast get to do it?"

"It lasts until every child has had a chance to do it for as long as he or she likes. If Jacob stays for half an hour and makes a hundred handprints, then that's exactly what he needs to do. If Amelia comes for thirty seconds and makes one handprint, that's what she needs to do. Everybody's different. Set it up for no more than four children at a time so that you can converse with children individually, and above all, take your time. You have all morning if need be. When Ms. Bates finishes breakfast, she'll visit the children in the learning centers, and she will also be in no hurry. She can join each child in play and have extended conversations. No more drive-by interactions in this classroom. And you both are going to have to learn to talk about something besides performance objectives, whether you're visiting a center or leading a small group."

Ms. Kruczynski smiles at the "drive-by interactions." She knows exactly what Ms. Lute is talking about. But the performance objectives reference puzzles her. Ms. Lute anticipates her question.

"I mean, you have to stop asking about shapes and colors and letters and numbers and big and little and hot or cold. Talk to children about your family and your experiences. Tell them about your little girl."

"You keep saying you want me to talk about myself and my family. Why?"

"Because that's how children learn to communicate—to use words to share their experiences, and all of their experiences are centered around their families. And don't just talk to the *children* about your family. Talk to Ms. Bates, too."

"Okay. Now I know that I no longer work for this school system. I am no longer Ms. Kruczynski, and underneath your smiling face, you are not Ms. Lute but a visitor from another planet. If there is one rule we have had at this place since time began, it is that teachers do *not* spend time socializing."

"When time began we didn't understand that children learn to communicate by listening to adults communicate. We didn't understand the importance of communication skills to success in school. But we have known both those things for at least two decades, and in this one program, in this one classroom, and for this one year, we are going to act as if we know it. Do you know why the children of college-educated parents are so much more likely to be successful than other children?"

"Not really."

"Because they talk to each other as if they've been to college, and their children listen in. I have an entire staff of college graduates, but in the classroom, they all talk to children as if they've had a lobotomy. It's going to be very difficult for you and Ms. Bates to learn to stop talking all day long about performance objectives because it is so deeply ingrained in your practice. But if you and Ms. Bates share your experiences with each other now and then as one adult to another, it will help you build better habits in talking to children. Besides, I trust you."

> "*I* have an entire staff of college graduates, but in the classroom, they all talk to children as if they've had a lobotomy."

"You trust me?"

"Yes. The rule about no socializing isn't just a way to make sure that teachers stay focused on children. It also comes from fear that if teachers socialize they will talk about things that are not appropriate for young children. But I think that you and Ms. Bates are dedicated professionals. I trust you to make good judgments about your conversations, and I know that you are certainly capable of conversing while you take care of children. You spend almost the entire day multitasking, and you are quite good at it.

"Thank you."

"By the way, Ms. Kruczynski, I've looked at your college transcripts. I saw that you took an art appreciation class and a few literature classes."

"Yes, literature was going to be my minor, but I never made it."

"Did you enjoy your art class?"

"Yes."

"Who are your favorite artists?"

"The Impressionists, I guess."

"Well that's something you could talk about."

"Impressionism." Ms. Kruczynski repeats the word flatly as if in a dream. This is not how she was trained to be a teacher.

"It's just one small step in the campaign to raise the level of discourse in your room. You also know how to think and talk critically about books. So do it. Do it with Ms. Bates. Do it with children. Do it every day."

The comment about books brings Ms. Kruczynski back to earth. She has spotted a flaw in the plan. "This all sounds just fine— conversing with children, letting everyone do their own thing. I like it. I really do. But you left out book time. District policy says we have to read a book to all the children every single day. It's on the district-wide daily schedule. No matter what you do, you still end up with 'Clean up your learning centers and come to the rug.' We'll still have all the same problems with kids who don't want to come."

Ms. Kruczynski is not happy to point this out to Ms. Lute. She was really starting to like her new classroom.

"You are asking all the right questions, Ms. Kruczynski. You are right about the policy. We do need to read a book to every child every day, and the school district does have a required time of day for reading to all the children at once. So I'm going to take some heat for this one, because reading books is one of the best tools at our disposal to promote language development, and I am no longer going to let it become this dreadful tedious experience for children that it has become." Too late, Ms. Lute sees that she has offended Ms. Kruczynski, and before she can proceed, Ms. Kruczynski interrupts.

"I don't think it's so dreadful. I *like* reading books. And if it's so important like you say, why don't you want me to do it?"

"I know you like books, Ms. Kruczynski." Ms. Lute hastens to make amends. "I bet your little girl loves books, too."

"Melissa? Are you kidding me?" Ms. Kruczynski beams. "I'm not saying this just because she's my daughter, but she's so smart, she could be in my four-year-old classroom right now. We read together every night, and when she talks to her grandmother on the phone, she'll say, 'Mee Maw, have you ever read *Sylvester and the Magic Pebble*?' just like a grown-up, and then she'll tell my poor mother the whole story."

"I had a feeling you had a very smart daughter."

"That's right!" Ms. Kruczynski nods vigorously. "*Sylvester and the Magic Pebble* is recommended for five and up, you know, and Melissa won't turn three for two more months."

"That's truly amazing. But do you think she would love books if you made her sit down on a spot for fifteen minutes with her legs crossed and her mouth zipped instead of sitting in your lap? If she had to raise her hand before she could talk? If she didn't get to hold the book and turn the pages and point to pictures and talk about the story? If you were also trying to make another seventeen children pay attention while you read to her?"

"I understand what you're saying, but she's not ready for that. It's different for the children in my room. They're four years old, and they're getting ready for school."

"So when Melissa turns four, are you going to stop holding her in your lap while you read to her? Won't she still need that intimacy and that individual attention?"

"Yes," Ms. Kruczynski admits. "So will I."

Ms. Lute presses her advantage. "Don't the children in your classroom deserve the same quality of education that you provide for your own child?"

"Yes, I suppose so, but I just don't see how that's possible. There are only two of us and seventeen of them."

It is precisely what Ms. Lute hoped she would say. "Which is the best reason I can think of for instituting the child-choice play-all-day classroom. In the morning, after Ms. Bates has visited the learning centers, while you're still leading your group, she can go to the book center and invite the children to come read a book with her—but no more than four children at a time. They can sit next to her and on her lap just like they might at home, and she can read to them just like you read to Melissa."

"She keeps reading until everyone has had a chance to read with her, even if it takes the rest of the morning. She can switch up books if she gets bored. If every child has not had a chance to read, but it's time to go outside, either one of you can read outside, or you can read to children after lunch when they have rest time."

Ms. Kruczynski is thoughtful. "You've watched me read to the large group before. You know what a struggle it is. So sure, I'd much rather read books like this, but will Central Office let you get away with that?"

"Sometimes it's best to beg forgiveness than ask permission."

Ms. Kruczynski smiles. That is her philosophy as well.

"But I do need you to promise two things."

"Name it."

"Keep track of what you read and who is read to so if Central Office does ask, I can document that all children are read to on a daily basis."

"That's easy enough. What else?"

"Do not use books—or any other activity for that matter—to teach performance objectives. That will defeat the whole purpose of our little experiment. There's no point in doing this at all if all we do is teach author, illustrator, and title page. Read with no agenda whatsoever. Read like you do for Melissa. Just for fun. The same for making handprints, planting seeds—anything at all you do. No agendas."

Documenting Progress in an Individualized Classroom

"Wow. No more objectives. No more paperwork. This really is going to be fun."

"Not so fast on the 'no more paperwork.' If you are going to lead fun and interesting things for children to do all day, then you will still need lesson plans describing what those fun things are. I don't want to see performance objectives on the lesson plans, and I don't want to see a single performance objective written on a note—"

"Yay!" Ms. Kruczynski startles herself with that outburst. Now it's Ms. Lute's turn to smile.

"But I do want you to write notes about what the children say and do throughout the day—not just during your group, but in learning centers, mealtime, outdoors, walking down the hallway— just anytime at all."

"I knew this was too good to be true," Ms. Kruczynski says good-naturedly. "But you know, writing notes is one of the most time-consuming things we do. I'm not sure how it will jive with the play-all-day classroom."

"Do you know why I picked you, Ms. Kruczynski?" Ms. Lute asks.

"Because you knew it would make me happy to break the rules?"

"Well, actually, yes, but that's not all."

"What else?"

"I read your Facebook page."

Ms. Kruczynski had friended Ms. Lute reluctantly, but after a while had not given it a second thought. Ms. Lute had never posted anything or made comments. But now Ms. Kruczynski is experiencing some serious remorse. She cringes inwardly as she recalls the pictures she posted of her Halloween party.

Ms. Kruczynski was a mermaid.

"You know, of course, who it is that you write about nonstop on your timeline, who is the most well-documented person on the planet."

Ms. Kruczynski grins sheepishly. "Melissa."

"The things you write about her are hilarious; the things she says are smart and cute; the pictures are always funny and interesting. But here's the point: I could complete an entire developmental assessment of Melissa just from her exact quotes, the pictures and videos of her, and the things you write about her."

"Really? I never thought about that."

"Yes, that's why it's perfect. You've been able to track her development and her learning with no agenda whatsoever. And that's what I want you to do for every child in your classroom. Do you have a tablet?"

"An iPad."

"Do you mind using it at work?"

"Writing notes for kids? I guess not."

"That would be great. It's going to be a very long time before I ever talk the district into issuing tablets. I'd like you to write two notes for every child each week and take as many pictures as you like. Do the notes and pictures just like you do for Melissa— imagine you're sending them home to parents to post on their own pages—which, come to think about it, is not a bad idea— sending them home to parents, I mean. Don't worry about what a note proves about development or learning. I'll worry about that. But do it with the kids. As soon as they say or do something you want to capture, write it immediately, with them watching you. Read them the words; show them the pictures."

"I think that *could* be fun. Can Ms. Bates do it, too?"

"Yes, but not right away. I want her to see what you're doing so she can understand what we're going for here. It's going to take her a while to unlearn writing notes about performance objectives. Eventually, she can take over half the note writing, but my guess is that you'll keep writing just as many anyway, because it will be fun and because the children will demand it once you get started."

"So when *do* we get started?"

"Tomorrow."

"How will I explain it to the children? Shouldn't we ease into this slowly?"

"Not at all. Think of it this way: tomorrow whenever a child wants to do something, you're going to say yes. No reason to begin by saying yes a little bit. Just say yes. The children will love the new routine. You're always trying to round them up to get to the carpet. Tomorrow, don't round them up. They will be quite happy that you don't. And here's something else you'll notice right away. You're so worried that no one will participate in group, but when the classroom changes from 'I need everybody to come here and sit down' to 'I'm doing this cool thing, but only four of you can come at a time,' the dynamic changes completely. You'll be turning children away because they'll be so anxious to be part of what you're doing. You'll have children standing around

When the classroom changes . . . to "I'm doing this cool thing . . ." the dynamic changes completely.

your table, and Ms. Bates will have children standing around the book center waiting for a chance to join, and you both will be telling them, 'Go play in the centers, and I'll call you when there's a spot.' And they'll say, 'No you won't. You'll forget. I'm staying right here.'"

"Okay, then, let's get started," Ms. Kruczynski agrees. "I guess I'll just have to see how it works."

"Send me an e-mail if you have any questions."

"I already have one."

"Okay."

"If I don't do performance objectives, how do I teach about print?"

"Well, you're already reading books and writing notes all day long. And you can give children opportunities to use print almost everywhere. Have them sign up for their turn in group. Make birthday invitations in the dramatic play center. Write out the batting orders when you play whiffle ball. I'm sure you can think of lots of ways to use print in the context of play."

"I see. One last thing I've been wondering about during this entire talk."

"And that is?"

"How did you know I was still lining children up at the sink? I didn't do it while you were in there."

"Your children will give you away every time. What you were doing for my benefit was obviously not their normal routine."

"And how did you know about my cell phone?"

"How did I know? My dear Ms. Kruczynski, everybody in the building knows about your cell phone."

"Oh."

Amelia Changes Her Mind about School

One morning in April, Amelia walks into her classroom and gives Ms. Kruczynski a shy hug. "Good morning, Millie-moo," Ms. Kruczynski greets her.

Amelia grins at her nickname. "That's not my name," she reminds Ms. Kruczynski.

"Please forgive me, Amelia. I don't know why I keep forgetting your name. With what remains of my wits, I want to remind you of your options. There's Ms. Bates over on the carpet leading songs and rhymes, and I'm multitasking, greeting children while I supervise the bucket brigade over there cleaning the tables for breakfast. I think you'll have to sign up on the waiting list for that one. We ran out of sponges."

Amelia likes the songs and rhymes; she sings them in her car seat on the way home from school. But she doesn't have to go to the carpet. She can listen from anywhere. The bucket brigade is full, and anyway, she's not particularly fond of the rowdy boys who tend to gravitate to that job. She knows what Ms. Kruczynski is going to say next.

"And, of course, you can choose any learning center. You know, Amelia, you didn't finish your panel for our water lilies mural. Do you want to work on that?"

"I'll finish after breakfast," Amelia promises.

"Let me guess. Dramatic play?"

Amelia grins again. She nods her head.

"Okay. But don't forget that breakfast will be here in fifteen minutes."

"I won't."

Ms. Kruczynski surveys her room. It is happy and busy. The children on the carpet are laughing, singing, and dancing. The tables are scrubbed and rescrubbed. Only three children chose learning centers before breakfast. Jean Anne is at the easel. Like Amelia's dolls, the easel is Jean Anne's haven from crowds and noise. Carlos has decided to embark on an elaborate building in the blocks center. Because he has a tendency to scatter all two hundred blocks on the floor and then move on to another center, Ms. Kruczynski makes sure to go over some ground rules with him before he begins.

"I want to remind you, Carlos, of the importance of maintaining an orderly construction site," Ms. Kruczynski begins. "I know you peek through the chain-link fence where they're building those new apartments next door to your house. I'm sure you noticed that all the concrete blocks are stacked neatly in one corner and the lumber in another and the pipes in another. That way nothing gets lost or broken, and nobody gets hurt. Your construction site is the same. All your building materials need to be stored neatly on the shelf until you use them. When breakfast comes in the door, you can leave your building standing, but you can't come to the table until all the blocks are off the floor. Do we understand each other?"

Carlos understands.

When the morning meal rolls in, the bucket brigade washes their hands and sits down to eat at one of the tables. Ms. Kruczynski helps them pass the food and serve themselves. When the sink is available, Ms. Bates sends her children from the carpet to the sink two at a time to wash hands and go to the table while the remaining children continue with their singing. When the last pair goes to the sink, Ms. Bates visits the three children in the learning centers. In the block center, there is no sign of Carlos, but there is plenty of evidence of his activity. A building is half completed, and blocks are scattered everywhere. Despite his best intentions, he forgot himself and bolted for the table the moment the food cart rolled in.

"Ms. Kruczynski, I don't suppose you have any information as to the whereabouts of one Carlos Rodriguez, do you? It appears he's left town in a big hurry."

"As a matter of fact, I do believe this is him sitting right next to me. Mr. Carlos, will you please get your SAVE sign out of your cubby and place it on your building so no one will bother it? And while you're over there, will you also neatly stack the remaining blocks on the shelves as we agreed to in our contract? I'll make sure no one bothers your breakfast."

Carlos does as he is asked. Ms. Bates gets him started on the block stacking, calling his attention to the correct shelf for rectangles, squares, triangles, and cylinders. As he continues to work, she visits Jean Anne at the easel.

"Tell me about your painting, Jean Anne."

"It's my neighborhood."

"I can see the houses and the trees. What will it take to finish it so you can come have some breakfast?"

"I don't know."

Jean Anne is stalling. She doesn't want to go to the table.

"In my neighborhood there are some gorgeous flower boxes in

the windowsills of some of my neighbor's houses. Do you want to add some bright colors to this neighborhood and cheer it up a little bit?"

"Yes."

"Then put your SAVE sign on the easel and wash your hands for breakfast. When you come back your painting will be dry enough to add the flowers."

Jean Anne realizes she has been outmaneuvered again and reluctantly complies.

In dramatic play Amelia is oblivious to all the activity around her until Ms. Bates rouses her out of her reverie. "Have those babies had breakfast yet?" Ms. Bates asks.

"They're not hungry."

"They don't eat because you don't eat. You need to be a role model for them, Amelia, and show them how important it is to eat nutritious food. Why don't you bring the high chair over to the table so one of your babies can see what a good eater you can be?"

Amelia likes it when the dolls join her for breakfast. She comes to Ms. Kruczynski's table while Ms. Bates joins children at the second table. As usual, Amelia has eaten before she came to school and she is not hungry. Scrambled eggs are on this morning's menu, and Amelia is completely indifferent.

"So Victor, I see you're eating your eggs," Ms. Kruczynski begins. "That will keep you strong and healthy. Tonya's having a good breakfast. She'll have lots of energy on the playground. And Amelia . . ."

Amelia doesn't wait for her to finish. She takes a bite.

"And Amelia is showing her baby the importance of good nutrition. What a good mother she is!"

Amelia likes being a good mother, and even after she has taken the inevitable bite of eggs, she does not retreat to the dramatic play center immediately. She sticks around to enjoy the morning conversation. She never knows what her teachers might say next. This morning is no exception.

"Ms. Kruczynski, guess what I'm going to do after breakfast," Ms. Bates calls from her table.

"I've got a brand-new book to read in the book center."

"What is it?" Ms. Kruczynski is intrigued.

"*Where the Wild Things Are.*"

"Maurice Sendak, right? I read that when I was a little girl. It's hilarious."

"That's right. The wild things try to act so scary, but really they're very funny."

"Well, guess what I'm going to do!"

"Tell me."

"We're going to try to finish all of our panels on our Monet water lily mural. When we're finished, we'll put the panels together and it will cover an entire wall, like in the museum in France."

"I know you love the Impressionists, Ms. Kruczynski, but I've noticed that the children have chosen some pretty wild colors. It looks to me more like abstract Expressionism."

"I see your point. I suppose it is a genre of our own making. And by the way, how have you become the class art expert?"

"Google Images."

"Ah. Of course."

"What about Ali? What's he doing today?" Ms. Bates is curious.

Ms. Kruczynski checks in with Ali. "Did you bring some more pictures you cut out from magazines this morning, Ali?"

"My mama cut 'em out."

"Your mother takes such an active interest in your education, Ali. You are very fortunate. So you're going to work on your collage?"

"Uh-huh."

"Ali is still doing his Romare Bearden, Ms. Bates."

"He's a man who knows what he likes. Hey," Ms. Bates adds, "maybe this would be a good time to write a note about Ali. It's evidence of persistence."

"Let's take a picture instead. I think the collage is evidence all by itself."

Ali disagrees. "Write the note," he tells Ms. Kruczynski.

"Ms. Bates, will you do the honors?"

"I guess I have to since I brought it up. Come on over here, Ali, and we'll write it together."

Ms. Kruczynski turns her attention to her table. "So children, what did everybody do this weekend?" Ms. Kruczynski asks the gathering at her table.

"I went to the zoo with my daddy," Joshua volunteers.

"I used to go to the zoo with my grandmother," Ms. Kruczynski recalls. "I would beg her for treats at the refreshment stand until she finally gave in. It wasn't all that difficult, though. She enjoyed spoiling me. What did you like best about the zoo, Joshua?"

Five more children try to tell their zoo stories all at once. Ms. Kruczynski silences them with a wave of her hand. "Joshua has the floor right now, children. Let him finish."

"Monkeys."

"Somehow that doesn't surprise me. You're such a good climber, you could probably teach those monkeys a thing or two."

"You're right, Ms. Kruczynski. Joshua certainly is athletic," Ms. Bates chimes in. "But you know, I can't enjoy the zoo the way I used to. My favorite part was the elephants, but now that I know how intelligent and sensitive they are, it's no fun. I feel like I'm gawking at prisoners."

"Elephants are almost extinct," Amelia observes.

"Ms. Bates!" Ms. Kruczynski exclaims with delight, smiling warmly at Amelia. "Did you hear that? Amelia hardly ever says a word, and now suddenly she's a college professor. What do you think of that?" It's a sincere compliment, but like almost all four-year-olds, Amelia does not grasp the concept of metaphor.

"No, I'm not," Amelia laughs. What Amelia doesn't realize is that inside her developing brain, the concept of metaphor is gathering traction, and by having preschool teachers who use metaphors, she is learning how to use them herself. Her sixth grade teacher will be astounded.

Her sixth grade teacher will be astounded.

"I think her parents watched that PBS documentary about elephants with her just like we suggested, that's what I think," Ms. Bates says. "And they talked about it, too."

"Did you watch an elephant documentary with your parents, Amelia?" Ms. Kruczynski asks. Amelia nods her head. Ms. Kruczynski is delighted. "I love it when I recommend a movie and someone actually watches it."

The meal continues and the children disperse to their centers. Jean Anne and Amelia return to their activities, but Carlos has lost interest in his building and visits the water table. Ms. Kruczynski takes a photo of his building and records a quote from Carlos about it. Then she sets up the water lily project at the art center table, where four children join immediately and three others observe, waiting their turn and taking in the flow of conversation. As the morning moves along, all the children have a turn reading the book with Ms. Bates and working on their art project with Ms. Kruczynski.

All of them except Amelia. She is lost again in her fantasy. Ms. Bates, however, will not be denied. She gets up from the book center and visits Amelia and her dolls.

"Amelia, have you read to those babies yet today?"

Amelia shakes her head.

"Don't you know that babies who are read to every day just for fun become the best readers in school? You don't want them to fall behind in school, do you?"

Amelia certainly does not want them to, and although she cannot express it, she appreciates that her teachers take her role of mother to this collection of babies so seriously.

"Look, Amelia! I have a book by your favorite author—Ezra Jack Keats. He's the same person who wrote *The Snowy Day*. This one is called *Maggie and the Pirate*. I bet your sister, Maggie, loves this book, too."

Amelia can't wait to get home and tell her sister. But for now, she arranges the dolls so they can all see the book. The other three children in the dramatic play center crowd around as well. A splendid time is had by all.

After about an hour, the mural project is winding down. Sophia was the first child at the table, and she has never moved but has remained in frowning concentration the entire time, trying to get every detail of her water lilies exactly right. Other children have come and gone. Some have worked on their painting for a few minutes and have gone on to another center, only to return the next time a seat opens up. Conversation is ongoing and is sometimes about the job at hand, but wanders across many topics, as human conversations are apt to do. Some children do not find this project particularly engaging and have to be coaxed into it, but Amelia likes painting, and on most days she has participated in this project without an invitation.

"We're nearly ready to go outside, Amelia. Do you want to come finish your water lilies?"

"I don't want to go outside," Amelia responds.

Ms. Kruczynski laughs. "Are you sure? Remember how the violets make the playground look like a purple carpet. And today just might be the day our daffodils bloom."

But today Amelia is just not in the mood. She's feeling very comfortable where she has been all morning and just doesn't feel like starting something different. Amelia's reluctance doesn't bother Ms. Kruczynski a bit. She plays the mama card.

"Amelia, we've been sending your mother pictures and stories about our water lily mural all week, and you know how excited she is about it. If she comes to the classroom to see it firsthand, and your part of it isn't completed, she is going to be very disappointed."

Amelia knows her teacher is right. The water lily mural is the first thing her mother asks her about the minute she gets home.

"And today is our last chance to finish it. Open House is April 14, and that's tomorrow. Bring one of the babies over here so she can watch you work."

"Samantha?" Amelia asks.

"Samantha is an excellent choice. She was telling me only yesterday about what an art lover she is."

Amelia smiles wryly and shakes her head as she and Samantha join Ms. Kruczynski at the art table. "Samantha can't talk," she informs her teacher.

"I know, Amelia. I'm pretending, the same way you do. It's fun to think that Samantha might be an art lover, isn't it?"

"She is an art lover," Amelia says matter-of-factly, reaching for a paintbrush.

Chapter 7

Where Do We Go from Here?
Creating a Human Classroom

Ms. Lute, Ms. Kruczynski, and Ms. Bates are composite characters who represent a growing number of early childhood professionals who are dismayed at the sad state of early childhood education. They understand the relationship between communication skills and success in school, and they recognize the detrimental impact of school readiness goals and performance objectives on the development of young children. They care deeply about children and do not wish to see children's very precious time wasted while waiting for national and state policy to catch up with basic child development.

Like our fictional trio, innovative educators are creating human classrooms that are tailored to meet the individual needs of children, providing maximum autonomy with a minimum of hoop jumping. In these classrooms, children participate voluntarily in groups and regulate their own ability and comfort level to participate in social interaction. Teachers do not view individual differences as deficits that need fixing, but value children for who they are. In short, all children find themselves in an environment in which they are able to be themselves.

Better yet, classrooms that support individual differences also maximize quality time spent with children and provide numerous opportunities for authentic conversations that are not limited to performance objectives and that build the capacity of every child in the classroom to communicate.

Nevertheless, the defining characteristic of state and federal early childhood programs remains steadfast devotion to school readiness goals and performance objectives, and innovators must be prepared for some very serious pushback. Chief among the objections will be lack of accountability. To many bureaucrats, Ms. Kruczynski's classroom and others like it seem to be places where adults and children just hang out aimlessly and talk about elephants and water lilies.

Redefining Accountability

Ms. Lute also wants her teachers to be accountable for how they spend time with children, and she wants her results to be measurable, but she looks at accountability differently. The best way to understand her thinking is to look at how childhood obesity has been addressed in early childhood programs. Young children from low-income homes are not only beginning school far behind their competitors in communication skills, they are also measurably less healthy. Measurements of body mass index have demonstrated that obesity is epidemic in low-income populations and that very young children are at risk for a lifetime of weight-related health problems, beginning with pediatric diabetes and moving into high risk for stroke and heart disease as they grew older.

The response of the medical and educational community has been to alter the nutrition choices offered at school. Accountability has not been accomplished by measuring the incremental weekly weight loss of each child. It has been accomplished by measuring what adults make available to children—by measuring and closely monitoring the amount of fat, sugar, and sodium in food provided by schools, preschools, and Head Start.

Ms. Lute believes that the science of language acquisition is as sound and as measurable as the science of nutrition. Since we know the quality and quantity of language that children are provided early in life determines their life-long ability to communicate, then accountability can be provided not by measuring incremental language gains in children, but by measuring the quality of language provided by adults. What she needs, though, is a way to accurately measure adult language.

Accountability can be provided . . . by measuring the quality of language provided by adults.

She has some ideas. One could, of course, simply count words spoken by adults. Or one could determine on a daily basis the percentage of management talk children are exposed to. Ms. Lute was weighing those options and others when, at a county-wide meeting of early childhood educators, she overheard her counterpart, Ms. Murphy, from the county Head Start program complaining about a class. Ms. Lute was sympathetic.

"What class are they making you take?" she asked.

"Oh, not *a* class. *The* CLASS. It's an acronym for the Classroom Assessment Scoring System (Pianta, LaParo, Hamre 2008), and we have to use it on every one of our classrooms. What a pain."

"Use it?"

"Yes. It measures classroom interactions. Come to think of it, you'd probably be interested in it. Parts of it are very similar to what you're always talking about. I guess you could say you could use it to measure the quality of discourse in your classroom—and individualization, too, for that matter. "

"Wait a minute! You have something that can measure the quality of discourse? I am interested! Can I borrow it from you? I'd like to try it out."

"Well, yes, it will measure the things you're looking for, but, no, you can't borrow it. It doesn't work that way. Your classrooms have to be scored by someone who's trained and certified." Ms. Murphy saw disappointment cloud her friend's face. "I tell you what," she suggested; "I've got a whole platoon of reliable scorers, and we've just finished our first round of scoring. I'll lend you a couple of my people to score your classrooms."

"You would do that? Thank you."

"Maybe you could put in a word with the school district to get their speech therapists into our classrooms instead of us hauling our kids across town."

"Done."

When her last classroom was completed, Ms. Lute received a summary of her classroom scores that included, among other classroom qualities, the level of language provided to children in her classrooms. Ms. Lute had waited anxiously for the verdict, hoping, like the lapsed weight watcher approaching the scales after a long hiatus, that perhaps the numbers on the scales would contradict the evidence of her own eyes. Despite her own observations, nothing would be official until the numbers were in. Until then, there was always hope.

Not this time.

None of the scores were very high, but those dimensions related to rich discourse were dismal. At a loss about what to do, Ms. Lute had called her friend Ms. Murphy.

"How long has Head Start been doing this?" she asked.

"Oh since '08 or so, I guess."

"And how have you managed to get high scores in the quality of discourse? What's your secret?"

"Who said anybody at Head Start had high scores? We suck at this. I don't mean just my county; I mean the whole country. Some programs are so bad they've lost their funding. That's why we all hate it."

Ms. Murphy is too hard on herself and on Head Start. It is true that in 2013, on a scale of 1 to 7, the median score for all Head Start programs nationwide in the domain of Instructional Support—that portion of the assessment most closely related to the quality of discourse—was a puny 2.71 (Office of Head Start 2013), which is definitely in the low range and demonstrates dramatically how low the level of discourse is in Head Start classrooms. However, state preschools and child care fare no better. According to Robert Pianta, the cocreator of the CLASS, in an eleven-state survey only a mere 15 percent of classrooms demonstrated effective interactions between children and adults (Rich 2013).

"Well, then, what are you going to do?" Ms. Lutes asked.

"Pray that Congress quits making us use the CLASS."

Ms. Lute hung up more discouraged than she had ever been. Head Start had been trying for years to elevate the quality of discourse in its classrooms and, even under the threat of loss of funding, had made almost no progress. What could she possibly do that would make any difference?

Taking a Page from Albert Einstein

It is said that on the morning that Albert Einstein came up with the general theory of relativity, he sat upright in bed and exclaimed, "It *must* be the time." His generation of physicists already understood that speed and distance were relative—that they were different depending on the point of view of the observer. A flight attendant tosses a bag of peanuts to a passenger in the row right in front of him. The passenger believes he is sitting still, that the peanuts traveled about three feet, and that it took one second for the peanuts to leave the flight attendant's hand and land in his lap. But a person standing on the ground would say that the passenger was not sitting still but was hurtling through the air at five hundred miles per hour. The bag of peanuts did not travel three feet; it traveled the distance of two football fields. Distance and speed are relative to the observer.

But not time. If on the airplane it took one second for the peanuts to arrive, then obviously, so said the physicists, it took one second for the person on the ground to observe it. Time is constant, they maintained. Not so, said Einstein. Actually, to the observer on the ground, it took a nanosecond longer for the peanuts to arrive than it did for the passenger. Two human beings, experiencing the exact same event, did so in different amounts of time. Time, said Einstein, is relative. The faster the airplane travels, the greater the difference in time between the passenger and the observer. As the plane approaches the speed of light, time almost comes to a complete halt for the passenger.

When he made his discovery, the evidence was in plain sight for any physicist to see. Einstein's genius was his ability to fearlessly reject the accepted scientific dogma of the day and thereby revolutionize modern physics.

Early childhood education is in a similar position. We have the evidence of how young children learn and develop right in front of us, yet we cling to school readiness standards and data analysis as if simply believing in them would somehow make them work.

On the morning she was scheduled to observe in Amelia's classroom, Ms. Lute defied conventional wisdom as well. Sitting upright in bed, she exclaimed, "It *must* be the performance objectives," and thus began her bold experiment. In April, on the day Amelia and her classroom finished their Monet water lilies, Ms. Lute had the classroom scored again using the CLASS instrument. The scores came back in the high range across every dimension, including language.

> *"I told them to forget completely about performance objectives and to talk to children like people."*

Ms. Murphy was astonished when she heard the news. "How did you do it?"

"I told them to forget completely about performance objectives and to talk to children like people. It took them a while, but they finally got the hang of it."

"I'd get fired if I did that," she marveled.

"I might be myself," Ms. Lute replied, "but I don't think so."

Ms. Lute did not get fired, but many objections were indeed raised to the human classroom.

But What If . . . ?
A List of Anticipated Objections and Responses

Objection: School readiness goals and performance objectives are mandated by state and federal policy. It is totally inappropriate to tell staff to "forget about them."

Response: There is no requirement that staff *think* about school readiness goals and performance objectives. Teachers do a much better job supporting school readiness when they are *not* thinking about them because their interactions are no longer confined to incremental, isolated skill building.

Objection: Progress must be assessed on an ongoing basis and tracked. Writing notes "with no agenda" is unacceptable.

Response: The most accurate and complete record of a child's performance is obtained when performance is observed and recorded throughout the day in different contexts and in different settings. When teachers focus on performance objectives only, they tend to record performance during teacher-led groups almost exclusively. Notes become a very simplistic record of how the child responds to an instruction or a question posed during a structured activity, and each record focuses on only a single performance objective.

Unscripted notes, written with the child, provide opportunities for print-rich and language-rich interactions. Each note is a treasure trove of raw data that contains evidence of progress across several developmental and early learning domains. Teachers do not reference school readiness as they write the notes but do so after the fact during their planning time, documenting the many domains and performance objectives implicit in each note and entering these milestones into the agency database. More notes are written when teachers "forget" about performance objectives because teachers see them as opportunities to extend their interactions with children rather than curtail them. Progress toward school readiness is therefore more thoroughly documented using unscripted notes that capture child development and early learning throughout the day and in all settings.

Objection: The daily schedule must be followed. It is designed to ensure that all required instruction and curricula experiences are included in the daily routine, that meals are provided according to USDA and licensing guidelines, that time spent outdoors and in learning centers meets minimum requirements, and that the amount of time spent in teacher-directed groups is appropriate. The so-called daily schedule developed by Ms. Lute keeps children in groups for up to two hours. There is no predictable routine, and there is no way of knowing if required curriculum is, in fact, implemented.

Response: All of the above is included in the highly individualized schedule. All required curricula activities are implemented, and all required experiences, including experiences with print, are provided. The participation of every child in every group is documented. The amount of time provided for child-directed experiences far exceeds the minimum requirement. Group time does not *last* two hours but is *available* all morning for very small groups of children, so that every child can work hands-on with materials and interact intimately with the teacher. The routine is quite predictable and is driven by child choice.

Objection: Parents don't understand the importance of social-emotional development or rich discourse. They expect classrooms to focus on academics.

Response: This is a classroom that honors and supports the pivotal role of the parent in preparing children for success. It is a classroom that understands that the language gap between children from low-income homes and more affluent homes cannot be bridged in a classroom setting alone no matter how rich in language. It is the responsibility of the program not just to build language-rich classrooms but to build language-rich homes.

It is the responsibility of the program not just to build language-rich classrooms but to build language-rich homes.

Enhancing the School-Home Relationship

In the standards-driven classroom, parents find weekly "home-work" assignments in their children's backpacks that communicate to them that school readiness is simply a matter of mastering performance objectives. For example, during any given school year, a parent might be asked to work with her child on printing her name, counting to ten, naming shapes, and identifying colors, alphabet letters, authors, and illustrators. Or, like poor old Scotty's mother, the school might worry that the child can't remember his own name and will instruct the parent to have the child recite his full name, address, and phone number every day.

The human classroom, however, represents a sea change in the relationship between school and home. Parents are no longer called upon to support the school in teaching performance objectives, nor are they judged by their participation or lack thereof in the home-work assignments provided by the school. Instead, parents are told very candidly about the enormous advantage that many children from higher income homes have in this cutthroat competition we call school. (Humans are, of course, complex, resilient, and unpredictable creatures, and many children from low-income homes beat the odds and excel in school. It is not our task to hope for miracles, however. It is our task to even the odds.) The language-rich pre-school can make up a small portion of that lost ground, families are informed, but the real difference must occur in homes. Families are empowered and provided tools to make changes in their daily lives that will enrich discourse in their homes.

For example, families of children enrolled in Ms. Kruczynski's classroom will find homework assignments that give suggestions such as the following:

• Tell your child a story about your own childhood every day.

- Tell your child a story of when he or she was a baby every day.
- When your child comes home, don't ask your child what she or he did or learned in school today. Instead, tell your child about what *you* did today—chores, errands, TV shows, visitors, telephone conversations—everything that happened all day long. Tell your child about anything you heard about on TV or online that interests you, or any family news you might want to share. Tell your child what you think about these things and how you feel about these things. In no time at all, without being asked, your child will start doing the same thing back to you—describing his or her entire day—because you have shown him or her how to do it.
- When you watch TV, talk to your child, your partner, your parents, or your friends about what you saw. Watch documentaries on TV every now and then.
- Take your child to the grocery store with you and talk to your child about everything on your list—where it is in the store and why you chose that particular item. For example, "Let's go to the dairy section because we're out of milk. We like 2 percent because it's better for us, and we're buying the store brand because it's just like the more expensive brand only cheaper. I think we can get by with a half gallon."
- Read to your child every day just for fun.
- Read things that interest you: books, magazines, web pages, newspapers. Talk to your child, your partner, your parents, or your friends about what you read.

Adult family members with mobile phones (almost all of them at this point) also receive at least two text messages a week plus a number of digital photographs about the things their children say or do in school. Parents and adult family members are encouraged to participate in the following ways:

- Read your cell phone messages from school (or your written notes) out loud with your child on the day you receive them. Ask your child to tell you more about the messages and the pictures.
- Send us messages and photos about the things your child says and does at home. Make sure your child gets to see the messages and photos before you send them. We'll show them to your child again at school and ask him or her to tell us more about it.

When programs partner with families to build daily habits that enrich discourse, adult family members see that it is not a ten-minute lesson that prepares their children for school, but rather everything they say and do when they are not teaching a lesson that has the greatest impact on their child's success.

Additional Objections That May Be Raised

There will likely be other objections to the human classroom that are less about bureaucratic requirements and more about how families in poverty are perceived by those responsible for providing services to those families. Such objections will include these:

Objection: Children raised in poverty experience chaos and trauma in their daily lives. They are not prepared to deal with a more open-ended schedule or the level of autonomy provided in classrooms such as Ms. Kruczynski's. These children will respond with disruptive, aggressive behavior that can only be prevented by a more structured and controlled environment. It's not that the classroom envisioned by Ms. Lute is not sound in its approach to child development; it is just much better suited to children from more stable middle-income homes.

Response: When early childhood professionals characterize the daily lives of children in poverty as chaotic and traumatic, it frequently conjures images of homes plagued by alcohol abuse, street drugs, domestic violence, and abusive parenting. To be sure, these are serious problems in any home, but they are certainly not bounded by income bracket. The chaos and trauma experienced by families who have no money is quite different than that experienced by families who do. For example, a child living in poverty may show up at his preschool classroom the morning after his family was evicted from their home because they couldn't pay the rent. He may have awakened in the middle of the night to a freezing cold bedroom because his heat was cut off. The police may have shown up at suppertime and led his mother away in handcuffs because she wrote bad checks for rent, heat, and groceries.

But a child who endures this kind of chaos and trauma does not need an institutional environment that believes it can provide security by providing rigid, school-like structure. He needs a human, responsive classroom that will provide emotional support, acceptance, and the security of knowing that he belongs.

Objection: Discussions of Impressionism, Romare Bearden, and PBS documentaries are much better suited to children from more affluent homes. To meet the needs of children in poverty, early childhood programs must focus on the fundamentals, particularly decoding print and numeracy. That is why we have performance objectives and that is why we track them, so that no child will enter kindergarten unprepared for success.

Response: Sean F. Reardon, professor of education and sociology at Stanford University, has this to say about what he identified as the widening disparity between children from even middle-income homes and more affluent children.

> The academic gap is widening because rich students are increasingly *entering kindergarten much better prepared to succeed in school* than middle-class students [emphasis mine] . . . High-income families are increasingly focusing their resources . . . on their children's cognitive development and educational success. (2013)

If children of more affluent families are showing up in school even more well prepared than even their middle-income counterparts, then there is something more at play here than the natural advantage of language-rich homes. These children are attending exclusive private preschools that care not a bit about school readiness goals or performance objectives, but do care about providing highly individualized hands-on, developmentally appropriate, language-rich experiences. They will, in fact, paint Monet's water lilies. They will investigate the fate of elephants. They will plant gardens, build tree houses and lofts, make murals, design terrariums, assemble dioramas, build castles and cities, play games, create Cornell boxes, paint, dance, make 3-D maps, prepare food, and sing. Teachers will relax and talk to children in ways that are natural and authentic. They will tell stories about their families, their lives, and their childhoods, stories about what they had for supper and where they go shopping. They will share their feelings, their ideas, and those things they care most about and those that bring them the greatest joy. In these kinds of schools, in classrooms not bound by rigid routines designed to replicate "school," books will be read to children in intimate settings for the sheer joy of it.

It is interesting to note that current federal and state school readiness standards have been written for and applied almost exclusively to children from low-income homes. Evidently, children served by these programs are not capable of processing rich discourse.

We have been taking this approach for nearly two decades, and if it represented best practices in the field, one would assume there would have been a narrowing achievement gap, not the growing disparity described by Sean Reardon.

Take the results of third-grade standardized tests in any school district in the country. Look at the students at the bottom—those who fall below the twenty-fifth percentile—and bet ten dollars on each child that she comes from a low-income home. You won't win every time—human beings are remarkably resilient creatures—but you will make a lot of money. Do the same thing for the top 25 percent, only bet that their income is 200 percent of the poverty level or higher. Buy a wheelbarrow to take home all your winnings. Make identical bets that the bottom 25 percent are children of color and that the top 25 percent are white. Buy another wheelbarrow.

As long as income and color are the most reliable predictors of success in school, then the field of early childhood education has failed its children miserably.

Some would argue that performance on third grade standardized tests is too narrow a definition of success. Longitudinal studies (Schweinhart et al. 2005) have identified other lifelong benefits of early childhood education, including statistics that show that the children of poverty who attend early childhood programs are less likely to be unemployed, less likely to be incarcerated, and less likely to remain in poverty than children who had no early childhood education.

That's good news, sort of. But if African American males who attended preschool are slightly less likely to be incarcerated than those who did not, is that what we're willing to settle for? Shouldn't we be asking why people from poor families and people of color are more likely to be incarcerated in the first place? Notice that no one touting the benefits of preschool for children from low-income homes wants to compare their success with that of more affluent children. They only want to show incremental improvement over children who have nothing at all. By presenting preschool as a solution to social ills such as unemployment, poverty, and incarceration, we distract attention from the painful but necessary discussions of race and class that must take place in order to address these issues honestly and productively.

Here's a study no one's ever done. Let's look at the incarcerated population to see if those who are released early for good behavior are more likely to have attended preschool. If so, should we give ourselves a pat on the back?

Putting School Readiness Goals and Performance Objectives Where They Belong

It is way past time for state preschools and Head Start to issue instructions to every single early childhood program in the country to open their laptops, start hitting the Delete button, empty the recycle bin, fire up the paper shredders, and erase from consciousness and memory school readiness goals and performance objectives.

Or perhaps we should not destroy *all* traces of this failed experiment. We could keep one copy of each set of school readiness goals and one of each set of performance objectives and place them where they rightfully belong, right between the Mercurochrome and the paregoric exhibits in the Museum of Stupid Things We Once Did to Children. In order to be responsive to the funding sources that demand school readiness goals, we could offer a single universal school readiness goal for each and every early childhood program.

If exposed to language-rich experiences, the child will
• learn more than we can possibly imagine;
• learn faster than we can ever hope to predict; and
• learn in ways more deeply contextualized and more broadly applicable than we could ever begin to track.

There is a Head Start program in Washington DC, Northeast, located in a public housing authority. The first thing the visitor notices when he walks in the door is the armed guard who greets him. When the children leave their classrooms for outdoor play, they are escorted by the armed guard, but they do not stop at the housing authority playground—perhaps it is the obscene language spray painted on the equipment; perhaps it is the whiskey bottles and drug paraphernalia scattered about. They walk two blocks with their police escort to the relative safety of a school playground.

After the visitor has observed for an hour or so, he has a question. There are three classrooms in this building, including the one up front that every visitor, parent, and staff person must walk right through in order to access the offices and the other classrooms in the building. There is also an empty room in the back of the building.

"Why," the visitor asks, "don't you use the room in the back as a classroom instead of the front room, so that people don't have to use the classroom as a hallway all day long?"

"The windows," he is told.

"The windows?"

"Yes. The back room used to be a classroom until the day a couple of bullets came crashing through the back windows and lodged in the far wall. It was a miracle no one was hit."

So is it true that entire neighborhoods have been decimated by drugs and the War on Drugs? Sure. Are they often without resources and support? Do residents fear for their safety? Yes. And is that Head Start center a refuge of sorts? Yes.

Nevertheless, there is also an interesting subtext to comments about chaos and trauma made by folks who cite that as a reason for not providing more individualized, more emotionally supportive classrooms or for focusing on "fundamentals" for children who live in those neighborhoods. It is a subtext that equates poverty with being less able to learn, with being less able to control one's behavior. It is a subtext that says an education that includes discussions of art and books is wasted on children who are poor and is more appropriate for the children of privilege.

But in those same decimated neighborhoods, against all odds, parents still raise families. Mothers love their babies. Parents in these neighborhoods have the same hopes and dreams for their children as do their more affluent counterparts. There is no difference in the potential of the developing brain of a child born in Washington DC, Northeast, or a child born in Georgetown. It is the obligation of every person in the United States to ensure that the children of poverty are provided the experiences that will allow every child to reach that potential.

So let's throw out standards-driven, data-driven early childhood education and focus instead on building communication skills that last a lifetime. Let's create human, caring environments that support the needs of every single child.

It's the right thing to do.

References

Barnett, W. Steven, Megan Carolan, Jen Fitzgerald, and J. H. Squires. 2012. *The State of Preschool 2012: State Preschool Yearbook*. New Brunswick, NJ: National Institute for Early Education Research. Accessed March 16, 2014. http://nieer.org/publications /state-preschool-2012.

Bruer, John. 2014. "Neural Connections: Some You Use, Some You Lose." James S. McDonnell Foundation. Accessed September 2. www.jsmf.org/about/j/neural_connections.htm.

Center on the Developing Child. 2007. *The Science of Early Childhood Development*. InBrief. Harvard University. Accessed September 2, 2014. http://developingchild.harvard.edu/download_file/-/view/64.

Chavous, Kevin P. 2012. "Why Are Prisons More of a Priority Than Schools?" *Huffington Post*, August 20. Accessed September 3, 2014. www.huffingtonpost.com/kevin-p-chavous/why-are-prisons-more -of-a_b_1611956.html.

Copple, Carol, and Sue Bredekamp, eds. 2009. *Developmentally Appropriate Practice in Early Childhood Programs Serving Children from Birth through Age 8*. 3rd ed. Washington, DC: NAEYC.

Covey, Stephen R. 1989. *The Seven Habits of Highly Effective People: Restoring the Character Ethic*. New York: Simon and Schuster.

Fernald, Anne, Virginia A. Marchman, and Adriana Weisleder. 2012. "SES Differences in Language Processing Skill and Vocabulary Are Evident at 18 Months." *Developmental Science* (December). Accessed September 17, 2014. doi:10.1111/desc.12019. http://psych.stanford .edu/~babylab/pdfs/FernaldMarchmanWeislederDevScience2012 .pdf.

García Márquez, Gabriel.1979. *Cien años de soledad*. Barcelona: Editorial Argos Vergara.

Hart, Betty, and Todd R. Risley. 1995. *Meaningful Differences in the Everyday Experience of Young American Children*. Baltimore: Paul H. Brookes Publishing.

Hudson, David. 2014. "Invest in US: President Obama Convenes the White House Summit on Early Education." *The White House Blog*. Accessed January 4, 2015. http://www.whitehouse.gov/blog/2014/12/10/invest-us-president-obama-convenes-white-house-summit-early-education.

Lally, J. Ronald, ed. 1990. *Infant-Toddler Caregiving: A Guide to Social-Emotional Growth and Socialization*. Sacramento: California Department of Education.

———. 2013. *For Our Babies: Ending the Invisible Neglect of America's Infants*. New York: Teacher's College Press.

Lonigan, Christopher, and Timothy Shanahan. 2012. "The Role of Early Oral Language in Literacy Development." *Language Magazine* (October). Accessed September 17, 2014. http://languagemagazine.com/?page_id=5100.

Marulis, Loren Marie, and Susan B. Neuman. 2010. "The Effects of Vocabulary Intervention on Young Children's Word Learning: A Meta-analysis," *Review of Educational Research* 80 (3): 330–35. Accessed February 14, 2014. http://sbneuman.com/pdf/marulisNeuman.pdf.

McGuinness, William. 2013. "Half of Recent College Grads Work Jobs That Don't Require a Degree: Report." *Huffington Post*, January 29. Accessed February 28, 2014. www.huffingtonpost.com/2013/01/29/underemployed-overeducated_n_2568203.html.

NAEYC (National Association for the Education of Young Children). 2009. *Position Statement: Developmentally Appropriate Practice in Early Childhood Programs Serving Children from Birth through Age 8*. Accessed January 19, 2014. www.naeyc.org/files/naeyc/file/positions/PSDAP.pdf.

National Center for Education Statistics. 2013. "NAEP State Comparisons." Accessed September 14, 2014. http://nces.ed.gov/nationsreportcard/statecomparisons/withinyear.aspx?usrSelections=0%2cRED%2c4%2c0%2cwithin%2c0%2c0.

Office of Head Start. 2011. *Head Start Child Development and Early Learning Framework*. Accessed January 5, 2015. http://eclkc.ohs.acf.hhs.gov/hslc/hs/sr/approach/cdelf.

———. 2013. "A National Overview of Grantee CLASS Scores in 2013." Accessed February 11, 2014. http://eclkc.ohs.acf.hhs.gov/hslc/data/class-reports/class-data-2013.html.

OECD (Organization for Economic Co-operation and Development). 2013. *OECD Skills Outlook 2013*. Paris: OECD Publishing.

Pianta, Robert, Karen LaParo, and Bridget Hamre. 2008. *Classroom Assessment Scoring System (CLASS), Manual, PreK*. Baltimore: Paul H. Brookes Publishing.

Reardon, Sean. 2013. "No Rich Child Left Behind." *Opinionorator*. April 27. Accessed September 18, 2014. http://opinionorator.blogs.nytimes.co/2013/04/27/no-rich-child-left-behind.

Rich, Motoko. 2013. "Language-Gap Study Bolsters a Push for Pre-K." *New York Times,* October 21. www.nytimes.com/2013/10/22/us/language-gap-study-bolsters-a-push-for-pre-k.html?src=xps.

Rose, Stephanie, and Karen Schimke. 2012. *Third Grade Literacy Policies: Identification, Intervention, Retention*. Education Commission of the States. March. Accessed September 17, 2014. www.ecs.org/clearinghouse/01/01/54/10154.pdf.

Rumberger, Russell W. 2013. "Poverty and High School Dropouts: The Impact of Family and Community Poverty on High School Dropouts." American Psychological Association. May. Accessed September 14, 2014. www.apa.org/pi/ses/resources/indicator/2013/05/poverty-dropouts.aspx.

Schweinhart et al. 2005. "Lifetime Effects: The HighScope Perry Preschool Study Through Age 40." HighScope Press. Accessed September 18, 2014. www.highscope.org/file/Research/PerryProject/specialsummary_rev2011_02_2.pdf.

Tabors, Patton. 1997. *One Child, Two Languages: A Guide for Preschool Educators of Children Learning English as a Second Language*. Baltimore: Paul H. Brookes Publishing.

Tyler, Ralph W. 2013. *Basic Principles of Curriculum and Instruction*. Chicago: University of Chicago Press.

Index